NUDES

A Search for the Invisible

NUDES

A Search for the Invisible

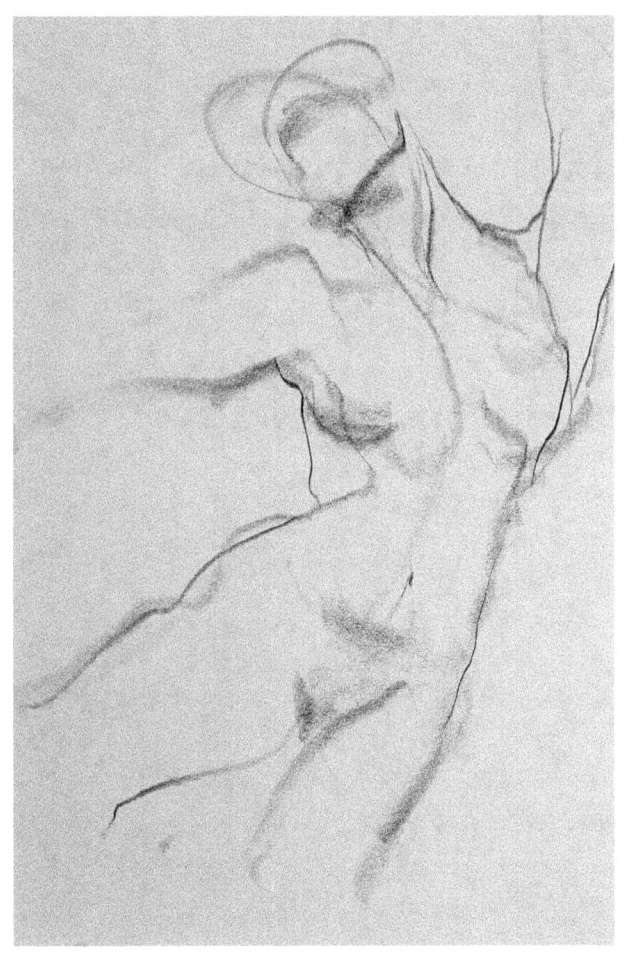

JOYCE EAKINS, M.F.A.

For

James West Black Brenneman
&
William Taylor Black Brenneman

Creators of the Future

CONTENTS

ACKNOWLEDGMENTS

My family, Pamela, Richard, Kate, Taylor, Jason, James, William, George, and Joan, are my underlying foundation. They provide the love and fulfillment that nourishes my life. Their creativity adds the spice that keeps me forever young. Family life is everything and it's never dull. I love you all.

The 23rd Street Studio is the place where I get lost. When I'm there I'm engulfed in the process. When I'm there I never want to be any place else. When the model steps into the pose the energy in the room is palpable. Beethoven, Bach, Leonard Cohen, Keith Jarrett, carry us into another realm. It's where I find myself on Monday mornings. Without the support of Michael, my studio friends, and the entire ambiance, my drawing would not be happening. I thank you all. I would especially like to honor the extraordinary people who come to model—performing artists, dancers, actors, artists, teachers, fashion designers, body workers—all professionals who take great pride in their work.

My profound expression of gratitude goes to my daughter, Pamela Eakins, whose keen perception, technical expertise, and hours of concentrated effort brought my words and images into a real book, and to my son and first reader, Richard Eakins, who, from a musical sensibility, resonated with my words.

Finally, I would like to thank Lou Solitske, a serious photographer and best friend, who photographed all the images and provided invaluable editing. Lou is a man in love with the two-legged, the four-legged, the winged creatures, and the planet we live on. For a decade he has generously given me his time, shared his energy, his humor, and his love of life. He has provided his technical expertise, his equipment, and his infinite patience, trusting that he could open the world of technology to me. Without Lou, what I'm doing would be impossible. I'm deeply grateful.

Before Thoughts

Every cell in my body loves to draw. When everything is working the immediate presence of the model causes my body to react like a tuning fork. I'm electric. I vibrate on a higher frequency. Consumed by the immediacy of the pose I'm no longer limited by my thinking mind. Nature speaks. Spirit rises. Soul ignites. Lines come alive. Yielding willingly to my heart, like a child I'm lost in the wonder of the moment. Wide open to whatever surfaces each drawing is spontaneous, unpredictable, not about something—*it is something.*

A blank sheet. A black crayon. A nude figure. The music begins and a lifetime of possibilities hang in the fold. Smudges, scribbles, scratches, merge into lines that lift-up to spirit, turn inward toward soul. Lines create holding space that waits in silence for impressions, feelings, reflections—invisible images felt not yet seen. *Rapt now—the moment is eternal.*

Drawer and drawn mirror unearthed potential that suddenly ignites in coherence. Empathy is the subjective source, the unseen force, the reflection that bridges all things. It's here/there/ everywhere—it's unconditional love that enlightens the way—*if I only see rightly.*

Drawing from the Inside Out

The spirit of the naked body hides in plain sight. Its uncovered truth never fails to captivate me. The immediate confrontation jolts me into a shared reality. I draw and mysteriously I'm drawn in. Slipping into the unknown, immersed in the process, lines, shapes, and forms automatically emerge. The drawing happens. Always a surprise, it's an impression of spirit seen through my heart—felt in my soul.

If I'm determined to make a good drawing it's sure to be a disaster, intellectually driven, technically as correct as possible, devoid of feeling. Knowing where I'm going imprisons me in the past. In the vitality of the moment there's no time for thoughts, intentions, or expectations. Diving into it demands risk. There's no longer a right way, or wrong way. Old rules and dull habits dissolve. Space opens. Magic happens. Soul reaches out. Spirit takes hold. Seeming to draw itself, the drawing comes alive. I'm in bliss.

Following my bliss, doors open, new paths appear, synchronicities happen, intuitive revelations surface. The inner depths are fathomless, the possibilities endless. I have barely scratched the surface.

The Invisible Reality

"The artist makes the invisible visible." Over 50 years ago that one sentence sent my mind into somersaults. I don't know exactly where or when it surfaced, nor do I know who made the statement. All I know is that it touched me deeply and launched me on a quest that continues to this day.

Antoine de Saint Exupéry writes in *The Little Prince*, "It is only with the heart that one can see rightly, what is essential is invisible to the eye." When my conscious mind told me to follow rules, I could only see and draw what I already knew. My feelings were blocked. The harder I tried I couldn't get beyond the surface. With my thinking mind in control I couldn't *see rightly.*

In every fairy tale there's a villain. In my story, the villain turned out to be my ego. In the process of drawing, the moment my ego got out of the way an intuitive circuit opened, I became instantly engaged. It took a lot of years before I learned the key was falling in love. Falling in love caused an immediate change in chemistry. A magnetic attraction happened. Love was the attracting force, the thread of connection, the bliss that opened the door. Only then could I make a quantum leap into the mystery. Seeing through the eye of my heart revealed the essence. *Love was the essence. Love was the invisible reality.*

Diving into the Dark

When the sun rises, when light first touches dark, a sudden flash sparks a new beginning. Light and dark resound. Past, present, and future come together. Cradled by the sun and the moon, unearthed potential rock and roll in universal rhythm. Ever-existing possibilities, conceived in the light of the eternal flame, become vaguely visible. Imprinted in the mystery original feelings, ideas, and images reflect in the dawning light. Something is aroused. Conception happens.

The allurement to dive into dark waters, to get through bewildering entanglements hoping to reach the other side—having touched my birthright—never fails to draw me in. I want both soul and spirit to speak. I want to catch the reflected images. I want to feel the light flood over me. To draw from life, to reach the invisible reality, to uncover, to disclose, to enlighten, and to rediscover something of nature's original intention, I must *see through my heart*. That's my impulse. That's drawing from the inside out. That's my task.

To uncover the forces of nature, first I must learn to understand my own nature. Each time I dive into dark waters something more of my own authenticity, my birthright, is uncovered. In the process my understanding broadens. I get closer to common ground where all life is interconnected. Eventually, I'll tune into deeper rhythms where soul is more than a whisper and spirit soars. The potential is there now—inside and outside, in darkness and light. It hides in plain sight—if I only *see rightly.*

Social conditioning often contradicts the natural feelings that rise inside of me. To follow my heart, it's necessary that I trust my own nature. It's then the doors open. It's then that synchronicity happens. It's then that I know I'm on the right path. There's no escape. I bump into it or it bumps into me.

Occasionally, when I'm sufficiently lost in the process, "It" happens—I'm in the *zone*. It's only in those fleeting moments, when light and dark resound, that the natural wonders—the imprinted reflections of the innate world surface. To get a brief glimpse of those forces requires letting go—being swept in. It's then that a clear connection is made with the model. It's then I draw from the inside out. The attraction, the connecting force that draws us together, is falling in love on an exalted plane. Here there's no separation. The harmony that ensues describes the interconnection of the nature of life, not only on this planet, but universal life. In truth—*we are one.*

Light and Dark

The light of the sun and the dark of the moon dance to the rhythm of the universe. Dawn and dusk, day and night, in continuous motion revolve toward opposite ends—*a new beginning.*

All my cats slept encircled in sun beams. I've seen morning glories open to early light. I've watched sun flowers follow the sun. Like other plant life the radiance of the sun nourishes me. It lights up my day. It warms my body. My skin drinks it in. It's so blindingly bright I can't look at it. All life on this planet is dependent on the light it gives freely—with no strings attached.

In Rome, stepping into the Pantheon, a circular building erected as a temple to all the gods of ancient Rome, I was drawn into a circle of sunlight pouring in through an ocular at the center of a massive dome, forty feet in diameter, wide open to the elements. In the light of that eye a surge of energy pulsed through me. I felt witnessed and empowered.

When I stepped into an environment created by the light artist, James Turrell, I had a weird feeling that I was being observed by an invisible observer. Enshrouded in darkness, without a solid wall to lean on, my sense of space had dissolved. I felt as wavering as a wobbly top—unguarded, ungrounded, and uncertain. Gradually, as my eyes adjusted, I was aware of a vague hint of light that soon appeared as a wall of light. I know that light has no mass, but my mind told me I had to test it. Now, I was neither trusting my convictions, nor my senses. With more than a little reluctance, I reached out. I went into the exhibit with the idea that I would view a light show and it turned out that I was the one experiencing myself experiencing and, freakier, I felt like I was being watched. Using light as his medium Turrell had shaken up my reality.

James Turrell believes that light occupies space and its presence can be felt. He believes it has *consciousness, knows* when we're looking, and *changes* as we look. I think that has been proven by quantum physics. Turrell says, "My work has no image, no object, and no focus. With no image, no object, and no focus, what are you looking at? You are looking at you looking. What is important to me is to create an experience of wordless thought." James Turrell has been working with light for over fifty years.

Without sunlight I'm enshrouded in darkness. With the flip of a switch I'm enveloped in light. Natural light or electricity lights up my picture. Photons strike my retina. Electromagnetic impulses act. My senses and preconceptions send instant inferences to my brain. After the information is processed the picture is snapped. The picture I saw and my perception of it are not the same. The result of unique sensing and conditioning—everyone snapping the exact same shot will end up with a different picture.

Light and dark are complementary forces. Light elicits spirit. Dark calls up soul. Light reflects. Dark absorbs. Enveloped in one I would never know the other. The degree of either in my lines and shapes determines value. My value scale ranges from white to black with as many intermediary changes as I choose. A sequence of subtle changes creates the illusion of form and dimension. Value creates mood, rhythm, harmony, unity, and balance. Juxtaposed black and white create contrast. Contrast results in tension. Tension creates interest.

Enveloped in outer darkness, behind closed eyes, my inner landscape is filled with light painted in colors poured in from somewhere—it's a *mystery.* In dreams—I see people, landscapes, interiors, and exteriors, in black and white or color—depending upon the story. Where does the inner light come from? Who are the actors? Who writes the scripts? Who is the cinematographer? Am I the painter, the writer, the actor, the photographer? Is the creator my imagination working overtime? It's a *mystery* to me and was to a scientist who changed the world. Late in his life, Einstein said he wanted to spend the rest of his life reflecting on what light is. Maybe Albert Einstein and James Turrell can connect on another dimension.

Body Story

Every body is beautiful. All life's experiences are recorded and overlaid forming the strata we are composed of. Layer upon layer of subtle gradations make up the fabric of each story. Every story, fleshed out by each added layer, has a unique outline. Time adds dimension. As I draw, I'm drawn into the truth in each story. Beauty is inherent in truth.

Every body has its own intelligence. After 13.8 billion years of adapting to the complexity and changes in life our brains are still in the process of transforming. I'm amazed at the capability of each cell to function alone, or to interact with other cells. The skeleton is an elegant sculpture supporting the body. I'm awed by the engineering feats of the working muscles. The breath creates an undulating movement through the spine. The expansion and contraction of each inhale and exhale gently massages the inner organs. Like a symphony, each organ plays its music in rhythm and harmony with the beat of the heart. Inexplicable chords create vibrations, threads of connection, back through our ancestry, back to that first cell. Nature's creation, the human body, is an extraordinary universal accomplishment still in the budding stage.

A new chapter in the Body Story is unfolding. The computer, the Internet, and the World Wide Web have revolutionized the world. Technological advancements in the last fifty years have changed the way I think, the way I act, and the way I live. A vast amount of information is at my fingertips. The push of a button opens a multitude of new possibilities waiting to be explored. Twenty-first century acceleration affects me physically, mentally, and emotionally. Adapting to change is not a choice—it's a necessity. New ideas are presented. Decisions are made. Action happens. This is life in the fast lane. And it's going to get faster and faster and faster.

Where is it going? What's happening to the human species? With the body as my vehicle and technology as the driving force, a shift into a relevant and timely mind-set is essential. My body is not the same today as it was yesterday. The cells in my brain are in a continuous process of adaptation. Can science and nature co-create? What new body story is evolving? My story is our story. Our story reaches back to the first flash of light. We're all made of the same stuff—all part of the same story. We're like a nebula, a large group of associated stars in an eternal process of creation. Each star is beautiful in its own way. Each is a work of art ever in the process of evolving.

Line

The powerful, unfaltering lines made by early man inside of caves some 40,000 years ago leave me awestruck. Overlaid images, with time spreads of 5,000 years, only add to their beauty. The Chauvet cave drawings near Avignon, in France, guessed to be 20,000 years old, fill me with wonder and envy. It's the authority and economy of line that makes these drawings masterful. The desire to replicate the magnificence of these creatures, rhinos, mammoths, lions, horses, must have been their way of honoring and respecting the spirit of such noble beasts—the source of their survival. It appears that they were the artists, the muses, the shamans, performing sacred rites—the cave their sacred space.

From aerial views, I see line drawings that blanket the earth like Jackson Pollock canvases signed by Mother Nature. Rivers reflecting the sun meander like undulating gold and silver ribbons. Wrenched from her belly, pitched in the air, jagged lines near perpendicular to the earth peak up to 14,000 feet angling off into table mesas with steep drops. Etched in rock walls cross-hatched lines black in their cracks disappear in darkness. Cone shaped craters spewing lava and hot ash, swirled and whorled into rivers of red lines that changed color in time. Windswept brown earth contrasts rough scribbles. Her vigorous nature creates marks of distinction. She is the source, the breath, the cause, the originator of earth graffiti. Mother Nature's gifts fascinate me—as I fly by.

I see imitations of Mother Nature's graffiti everywhere—lines in sand, lines on the bark of trees, lines inside of caves, lines in the most weird and unexpected places. During World War Two, "Kilroy was here," appeared wherever American soldiers had been stationed. In the 1960s in New York City, kids began to take pride drawing lines with permanent markers, or aerosol spray cans, in subways, on sidewalks, buildings, fences, windows, walls, or on any other public structure. It was against the law and became even more dangerous when they began marking trains and freeway overpasses with their nicknames and logos. The more risk involved increased their peer status. The writings and logos were visual marks that proved their existence and identified who they were. It was "underground art" labeled *graffiti.* Over time, their markings became more refined in style and technique and evolved into a new art form—*American calligraphy*—our newest Folk Art. The writers became recognized by the art establishment in both the U.S. and in Europe. They made their mark even though Mother Nature beat them to it.

The first line I drew was my inhale at birth. That line began my story. For as long as I can remember, drawing lines and scribbling shapes with crayon, or any other medium, on any surface has fascinated me. My line drawings, at age two, were on the pages of my mother's prized *Alice in Wonderland*—a gift to her in 1909. In graduate school, I was proud to submit one of those drawings into an MFA exhibit as my earliest drawing—at least I thought it was my earliest. *Alice in Wonderland,* with a few missing pages, is still on my library shelf.

When I was three years old, I remember being on my knees on the living room floor, crayon to paper, making my marks. Those marks were probably my first attempt at portraiture. My mother was outside. When she came inside her shrug told it all. That was my first rejection. The portrait looked exactly like her. Picasso would have been jealous.

When I entered the room on my first day of kindergarten, I saw easels with all the colors of the rainbow, lined up in jars on rails under big sheets of newsprint paper clipped to easels with clothes pins. I still remember how my heart pounded. The teacher told us as soon as we brought our daddy's old shirt we could paint. The next day I was the first to dip into the red and then the blue. I remember the thrill I felt seeing the lines of color running down and dripping off the paper. They were my marks. Thinking about it now makes my heart pound.

Jean-Michel Basquiat, one of the first New York graffiti artists, said, "I like kids' work more than work by real artists any day." I like his work and I like kids' art better that most art as well. Kids' art is direct, innocent, and honest—as is Basquiat's—except his has a *dark twist*. One of his paintings recently sold in an auction house in New York for $100.5 million dollars. There's no doubt about it—he made his mark.

Children's art is never involved with ego. When my ego surrenders my lines spring out of the deepest realms of sub-conscious. They are threads that connect to the model. Threads that signify life, energy, tension, force, action, impulse, urge, direction, movement. Each line, or its absence, is significant. A line extends a point. A line connects one thing to another. A line can lose itself and find itself again. It can be fast or slow, light or dark, active or passive. It can be aggressive, sensitive, sweeping, geometric, reaching, sinking, joyous or sad. The end drawing is an expression of two souls converging—*when my ego doesn't crowd in.*

Self-Portraits—Soul-Portraits

The instant my crayon touches the paper the mark I make reflects how I'm feeling. If for one second I think I'm not drawing well— I'm not. Judgment locks me out. Judgment walls off my senses. Judgment is about ego. If I can't relate to the pose, if the music is distracting, if I'm dwelling on something that happened yesterday, if I'm tired, cold or hot—all of those "ifs" are conscious diversions—divisions that keep the magic from happening. Each drawing exposes my state of being in that time frame.

When the process is effortless, when my conscious mind lets go, I draw from the inside out. When I draw from the inside out I mirror an image of the unseen world where soul lives. My thinking mind is bypassed. Soul draws—spirit rises. These drawings are *soul-portraits.* They're from the ingrained seed that determined the origin of life. They reflect something of nature's original intention, a pattern that evolved from the source common to all life. They're rare gifts.

If my ego hasn't crowded in—if self-consciousness has vanished— the circuit opens. I connect with the model. Two streams of consciousness flow into one river. The strength of connection, the measure of our combined sensibilities, determines whether the drawing is a self-portrait or a soul-portrait.

Waking up the Senses

Sensation is the body language of my emotions. Through my sensory organs, I see, hear, smell, touch, and taste. These organs are from the Big Bang, from the same seeds that made this planet, its atmosphere, and its light. They are my birthright. They are my doors and windows into the world.

The keenness of my senses is the means through which I access both my inner and outer awareness. Every day, I'm bombarded by a multitude of sensations, that depending upon my degree of perception, either heighten or diminish my sensitivity. Making sensitive choices and sifting out the rudimentary requires constant vigilance.

Falling in love with the sunset startles all my senses. I see it. I feel it. Suddenly I'm enveloped in it. Recently, standing in front of a Rothko painting, I was swallowed by red. It wasn't just red-red, it was the universe dressed in exquisite nuanced reds—blue-reds, yellow-reds, orange-reds, gray-reds, a multitude of reds. Many times, I've been swept into the beauty of an oriental carpet. Anything that excites me to the point of making my heart pound forces my attention. The emotions that arise affect my whole body. They stem from the experience I had walking into the kindergarten class—my sensory faculties were given a jump-start. At that moment a life-long urge was born. It was love at first sight

The ability to perceive people, situations, and things, both objectively and subjectively, depends on all my senses being alert, ready, and awake. Over time, as my responses are quickened and increase in sensitivity, my sensibilities will become more subtle, more nuanced, and more refined. I'm grateful for all the sensations that bring out the elusive qualities that unceasingly enhance my life. Without the use of my senses life would be without reason—*senseless.*

In the Zone

Whether serving a tennis ball, watching the sun set, looking at a Rothko painting, or drawing the figure—I'm swept into a new level of consciousness. Absorbed by the object, lost in "It," I'm here and there at the same time—in the *zone*. In the *zone*—body, mind, and spirit unite in *unconditional love*.

After Sunday dinner Grandad spread pillows out across the living room floor. Encouraged by smiling family, my sister and cousins, all between two and five, lined up to play follow-the-leader somersaulting over the pillows. In the summer he conducted races outside. When I was six years old, Grandad tied my sister's right leg and my left leg together for the three-legged race. When he said, "Ready, get set, go!" we ran like the wind. I learned with every sport I fell in love with that there were those magical moments when I was in the *zone*. Lost in the process ego dissolves. The first time I was *consciously aware* of that feeling was in the three-legged race. It was effortless—our feet sprouted wings. We were united—two in one—in *"It."*

In mid-life, I took up yoga, a philosophy and physical practice that unites body, mind, and spirit. In Sanskrit yoga means union. The postures taught me about the intelligence of the body. I learned to slow down, become still, and listen to the sound of my breath, the beat of my heart, and the blood coursing through my veins. I became aware of the subtlest changes—both inside and outside. I became consciously awake to the fact that I was more than the limitations of my physical body. The last posture in each session is a pose of complete relaxation. It simulates the experience of dying. Stretched out on my back, melting into the earth, I breathed into a sense of boundlessness. Body, mind, and spirit, united in unconditional love, dissolved into a sense of wholeness. In wholeness I felt holy. In wholeness I was in the *zone*.

Intuition

From out of the mystery, by-passing rational thought, images and ideas zip into awareness. Surging feelings, pressing questions, automatically light up the circuitry. Bypassing all five senses *intuition* answers the call and gets to the point. It elucidates insights embedded deep in my memory, things I know in my bones to be true, things seeded in the mystery. It might better be called the oldest sense. It's thought to be rooted in the quantum world before our solar system existed. In less than a nanosecond, answers, innovations, and revelations form in my consciousness. I get the whole picture in one shot.

When my daughter was less than two years old she had a fall. Her cry sent an alarm that skipped all five of my senses. Nothing visible indicated the cause of her pain. My need to understand was so intense—my concentration so pointed—it penetrated the surface *into the cause.* Telephoning the doctor, I heard myself say, "She has a broken collar bone." Emergency room x-rays confirmed the "intuitive" diagnosis.

Intuition isn't always brought on by drama. Sometimes, in the middle of a mundane task *out of the blue* I see something in a new light. At other times, I'm aware of faint or gnawing nudges, red flags, I've learned to trust. They tell me to stop, re-examine, or go for it. "It" is the point of connection, the balance point where macrocosm and microcosm meet, where past, present, and future come together, where solutions appear, where the mystery unveils.

Curiosity

Outside of time, transfixed by the unexpected, the innocent, the wide eyed, those with open hearts, those who wonder and dare to wander, are caught spell-bound. Confronted by surprise, lured by adventure, drawn inside of experience, the inquisitive as well as the childlike are struck by the power of the "sorceress." The author of *Alice's Adventures in Wonderland,* Lewis Carroll, described the captivation in these words, *"'Curiouser and curiouser'* cried Alice. She was so much surprised, that for the moment she quite forgot how to speak good English."

I must have been startled when I made my first impulsive mark in the *Alice in Wonderland* book. That moment of surprise surely must have fired my curiosity. I'm still captivated by the lines and shapes that just seem to happen. I draw, but it's curiosity that draws me in. I'm still becoming *curiouser and curiouser.*

Curiosity is an innate characteristic in everyone. Babies are naturally curious about their fingers and toes. Everything they see, hear, smell, touch, and taste excites their inquisitive nature, and usually ends up in their mouths. The moment a baby makes first eye contact with the vague image hovering above must be spellbinding.

In *The Wright Brothers,* David McCullough describes how a stick with twin propellers and a twisted rubber band, rubbed between their palms, excited the boy's curiosity. When they let go they were awestruck when it flew up to the ceiling. With it went their imaginations. Flight was the motivating force that later led Wilbur and Orville Wright to build a glider.

They became so absorbed in the flight of birds, the subtle movements of their wings in take-offs and landings, the birds became their teachers. Their curiosity took them to the library where they read books about birds, and studied the principles of aerodynamics. The result was the invention of a powered *flying machine.* In 1903 they made their first flight in the *Kitty Hawk* at Kitty Hawk, North Carolina. Flight changed the world.

When she was four years old, during a crossing of the English Channel, Margaret Burbidge's wonder about the stars in the night sky sparked a fire that never died. Her curiosity led her to become an astronomer, and later an astrophysicist. In 1973 at the Lick Observatory in California, her research proved the cosmic theory that human beings are made of stardust. Curiosity led her to many other scientific achievements. The National Medal of Science and The Albert Einstein World Award of Science are among the awards she has received.

For millennia, curious people from all walks of life, artists, scientists, philosophers, inventors, have been asking questions about life and the mysteries of the universe. The most important work of the painter, Paul Gauguin, in Tahiti in 1897, was entitled, "Where do we come from? What are we? Where are we going?" Questions unlock curiosity. Curiosity frees imagination. Imagination unleashes potential.

In *The View from the Center of the Universe,* Joel Primack and Nancy Ellen Abrams, addressed the same questions Paul Gauguin was asking—the same questions we all ask. They were not only curious about what we are and why we are—they shifted their point of view. Their questions were about the living universe and how we fit into it.

My curiosity and love for the human body, mind, and spirit, reflects a deep urge to *wake up*—to understand my purpose—and realize my place in the universe. If I get out of my own way and let the sorceress do her work—it's possible that each drawing can be a fresh adventure into a boundless sense of knowing. *Curiosity will lead my way.*

Imagination

Sparked by curiosity, the window of my soul unveils. Lured into the unknown, my imagination glides effortlessly into the mystery. Like a bird in flight, it soars high before dipping into a treasure-house of information—an accumulation of ideas and imagery, a collection from the earliest beginnings.

In a meditation group I was asked, "If you were reborn as a four-legged creature, what animal would you choose to be?" Captivated by curiosity—my imagination went wild. A succession of animals appeared. Quickly, I ruled out dog and cat—too tame. A deer appeared wary-eyed, ready to bolt—too skittish. Lions and tigers and bears—*bear!* When I was five I was chased by a bear—that ruled all three out. Even the graceful cheetah couldn't survive the cut. Finally, when I concluded that a two-legged creature was the only form I could be, my imagination took flight. Out of the blue an eagle appeared.

Soaring on the wings of the eagle—past, present, and future come together—transcendence happens. Acting on my imagination a new reality unfolds. Without imagination I would be stuck in the past—incapable of moving forward. Given free reign, morphing imagery seizes my consciousness, animates my creative juices, keeps my life fertile. Detached from the familiar, imagination is the eagle in flight, close to the sun, in touch with the earth. In a heightened sense of wonder, new possibilities are presented.

That eagle took form in a painting I called "I Could be an Eagle."

I am a Verb

I am a verb altered with each experience. I heard Buckminster Fuller utter those words at a conference in Aspen, Colorado, shortly before he died. A verb is a part of speech that expresses an action, occurrence, or way of being. My actions have resulted in an accumulation of experiences that are preserved in the bedrock of my being. What is happening in the present and what will happen in the future is based on past actions. My actions have made me who I am.

Every action necessitates change. Every action alters my experience. Accepting change and adapting to difference is to embrace life. It's an adventure in the unknown. It provides broader understanding and explores unrecognized potential. More potential presents new perspectives. New perspectives provide opportunities. Opportunities entail choices. Choices require decisions. Decisions determine resolutions. Resolutions result in evolution. Evolution is gradual change to a more complex form. When asked by the Caterpillar who she was—it's no wonder that Alice replied, *"O-I hardly know, Sir, just at present—at least I know who I was when I got up this morning, but I think I must have changed several times since then."*

If I didn't *wake up* I would never get out of bed. Awakening to the inner urge, the insistent prodding to do something, or to act on something, is to become conscious. The urgency to move, to turn, to revolve, to recycle is universal insistence, an irresistible appeal, the motivating force, the relentless cause that drives me to act— to do what I do. The passion that I feel equates with how awake I am—the level of "consciousness" I have achieved. It continues to evolve from the seed that was implanted at the time of the Big Bang. I do what *I can't not do.* It's my passion.

Consciously aware actions, reactions, changes, and adaptations—organized and coded—make up the complex of data alive in my subconscious. The lines I drew in *Alice in Wonderland*, the portrait of my mother, the Renaissance drawings in high school, education, skills, marriage, family, travel—including the ancestral memories engraved in my DNA—it's all there etched in the living layers of strata that form the underlying structure of *who I am.*

Evolution is a dynamic process—the result of action—spiraling, revolving, and expanding. Each revolution spirals on a slightly higher plane. Each revolution involves change. Each involves adaptation. The result is a keener awareness and a more discerning way of living. I am evolution. I am change is process. I am process in action. Action is life in process. Process is a continuum. Like Buckminster Fuller, I too am a verb altered with each experience. Like Alice, *"I have changed several times since I got up this morning."*

Content

Meaningful content comes from the mysterious world within. To see true nature, to make the invisible visible, I must see through my heart. Only then will I be able to touch that something, the *inner essence*, that will give the drawing universal content. To enlighten the many dimensions of inner life requires more than factual findings. Looking within, drawing from the inside out, takes emotional involvement. Each experience takes me deeper into *"It"*—if I see *rightly*.

To see through the eye of my heart I must fall in love unconditionally. Unconditional love is beyond my control. It happens. It has no restrictions, no expectations, no judgments. The instant chemistry creates threads of connection to anything—sun, sky, sea, birds, clouds, earth, the universe, or to the human figure. The interwoven threads weave a common cord that binds me with it. Seeing from a magnanimous point of view I tune into refined sensibilities that draw all life together. With no separation—here is there—there is here—two become one. Nature reveals herself. Something of the mystery is shared. *Unconditional love is the medium, the essence, the universal content.*

Editing

If I could touch the *invisible reality*—I could reach *the impossible dream.* To grasp something that isn't *out there* would be impossible. Not to try would be a betrayal of my heart. There is a twist. If it can't be reached by going *out*—the way to go is *in.* To go for "It" takes courage, perseverance, and spirit. *It's the way of the heart.*

Transparency is a prerequisite. History filtered, reveals the gold that reflects new light. Going within entails intense scrutiny. Obsolete memories, ideas, habits, and values—experiences collected and stored in the past—created shadows that obscured the light and left the path in relative darkness. It takes repeated sifting, straining, and refining to remove the irrelevant, to clean out the refuse, and lighten the way.

Positive space refers to visible matter: *form, body, contour, and structure.* It provides content and meaning in the drawing. Too many things create a mass of clutter that suffocates my drawing and my life. With no room to breathe, with no space for pause, the only recourse is to get out the eraser. Cutting, cleaning, clearing—refining, polishing and purifying—enable me to *see into the invisible reality.* Transparency inspires truth.

Negative space is not empty space. It's a mysterious place that catches the viewer by surprise. It's not a vacuous space. It's a holding space—a place to pause—to connect, to collect, to reflect, and to imagine. It's the space in between—the space around—the breathing room—where inspiration happens.

Striking a balance between positive and negative space is like walking a tight rope—it's a little shaky. Too much or too little of either destroys the effectiveness of the other. Surviving the sifting, straining, refining, altering, correcting, and defining— demonstrates true grit. The cutting-edge hones all my senses. Love can be tough. I trust my heart—it knows the way.

With transparency of purpose, with love lighting the fire, the invisible reflects more of itself in my drawings and my life. Editing creates space for truth to shine through. Editing reveals the gold. Editing is a lifetime process.

Landmarks

Looking at the figure is like looking at a map. The landmarks are obvious—head, spine, nipples—navel, crotch, hips—knees, ankles, feet—shoulders, elbows, wrists, and hands. The spinal column is the great highway. If I don't show it I need to know it. Lines connecting the landmarks suggest the component parts. A quick action drawing is how I get into it.

Quick Action Drawings

The model strikes a pose. I see it. I feel it. Without thought the wisdom of my body surfaces—muscle memory takes over. On paper, I sweep in the action of the figure. As sudden as it began—it's over. I wonder, "Who drew?"

The immediate challenge switches my brain off. If I don't lose myself instantly the pose is over. The purpose is to capture the gesture. Likeness is of no concern. I can't think it—I have to feel it. If I can't feel it—I can't draw it. To be one with the model, one with the gesture, one with the line, is being in the *zone*. In the zone time is eternity—now is forever. These drawings are fast, flowing, and fun. I love the process.

To Sink
1-2 Minute Drawing

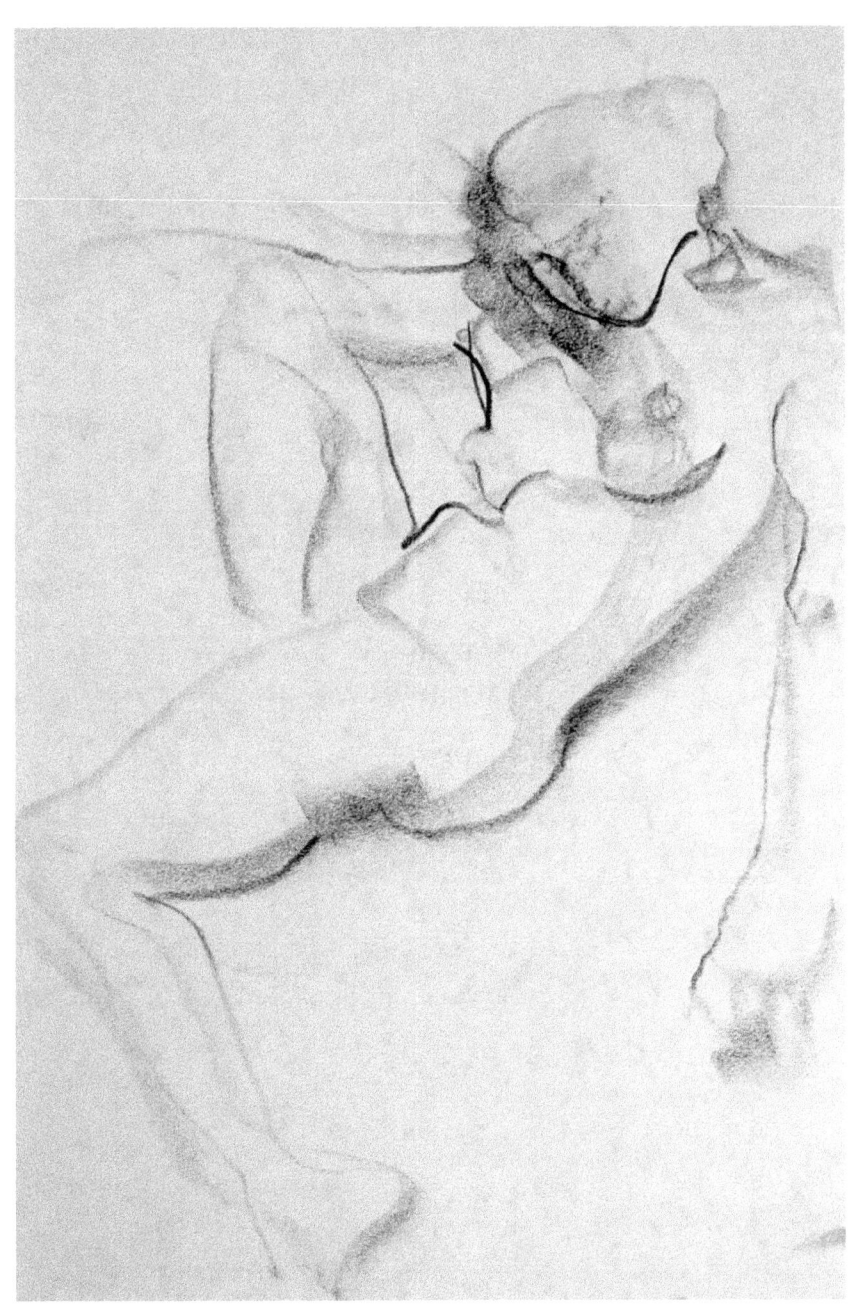

To Run
1-2 Minute Drawing

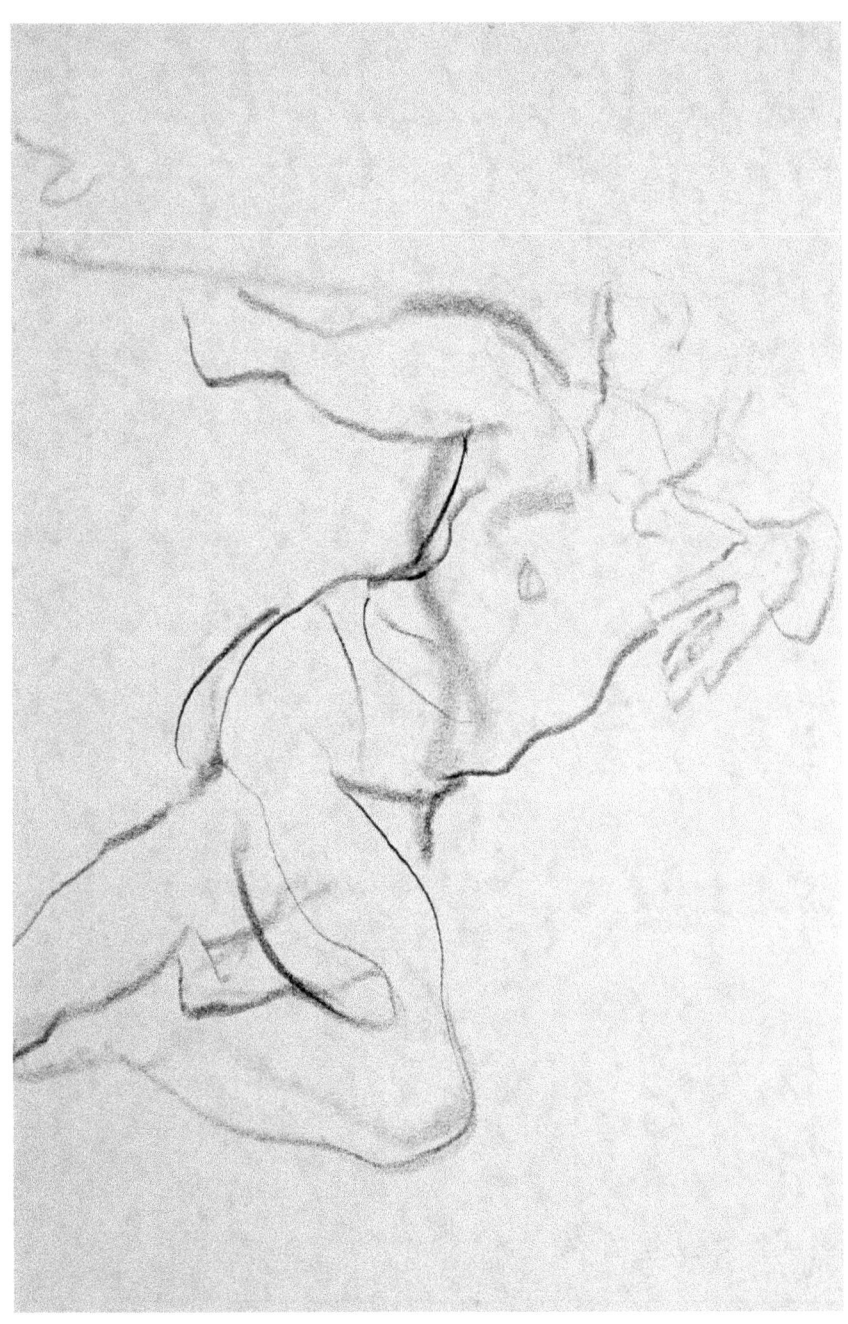

To Fling
1-2 Minute Drawing

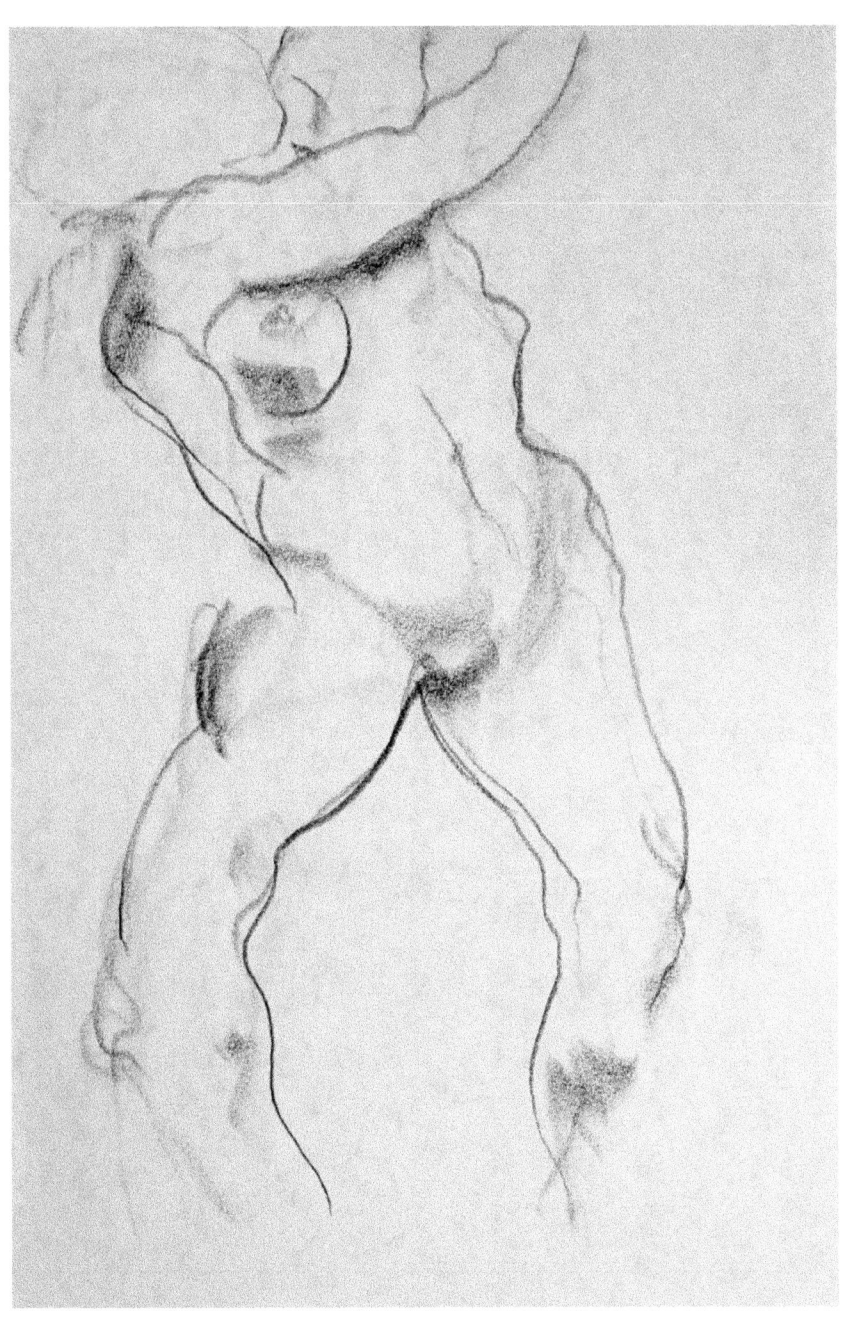

To Dance
1-2 Minute Drawing

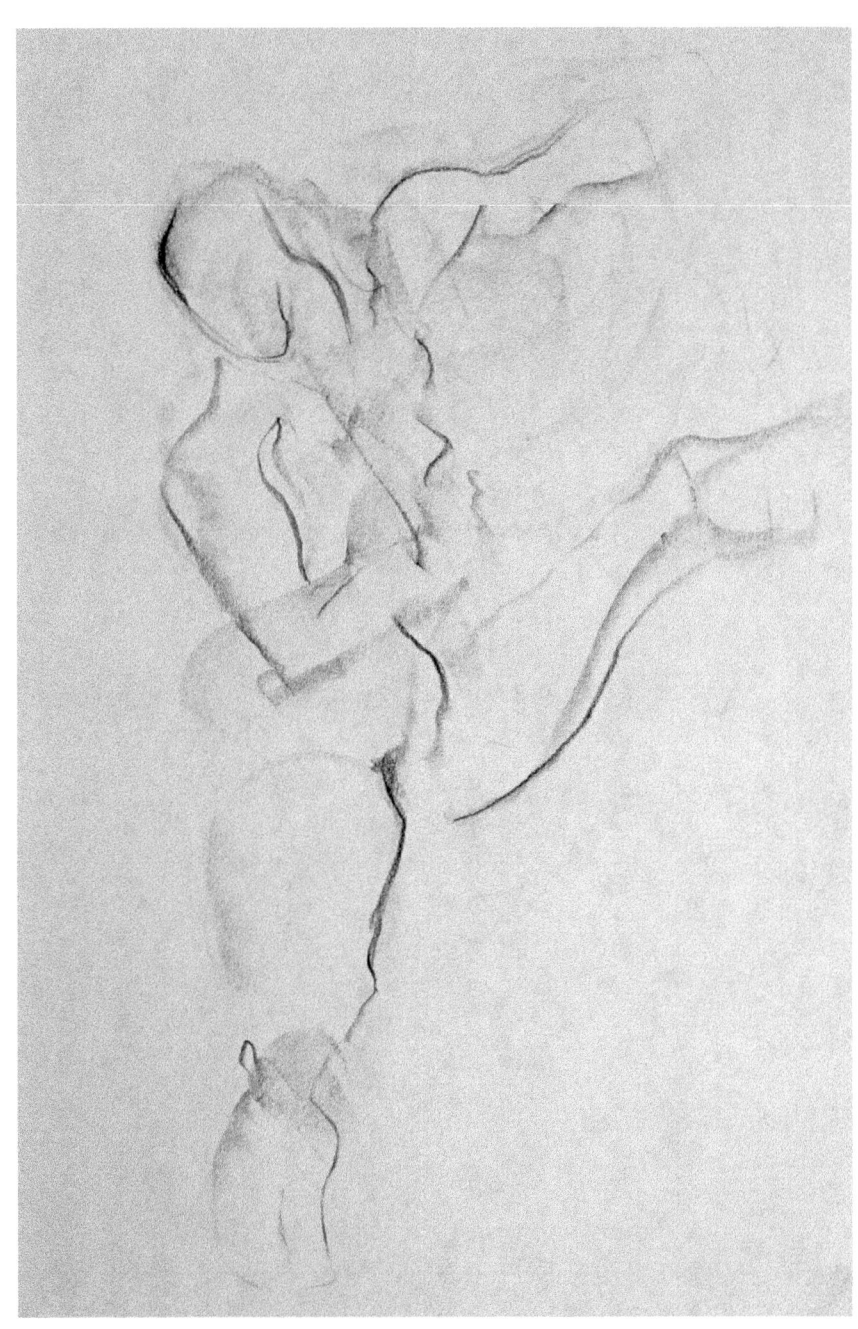

To Fly
1-2 Minute Drawing

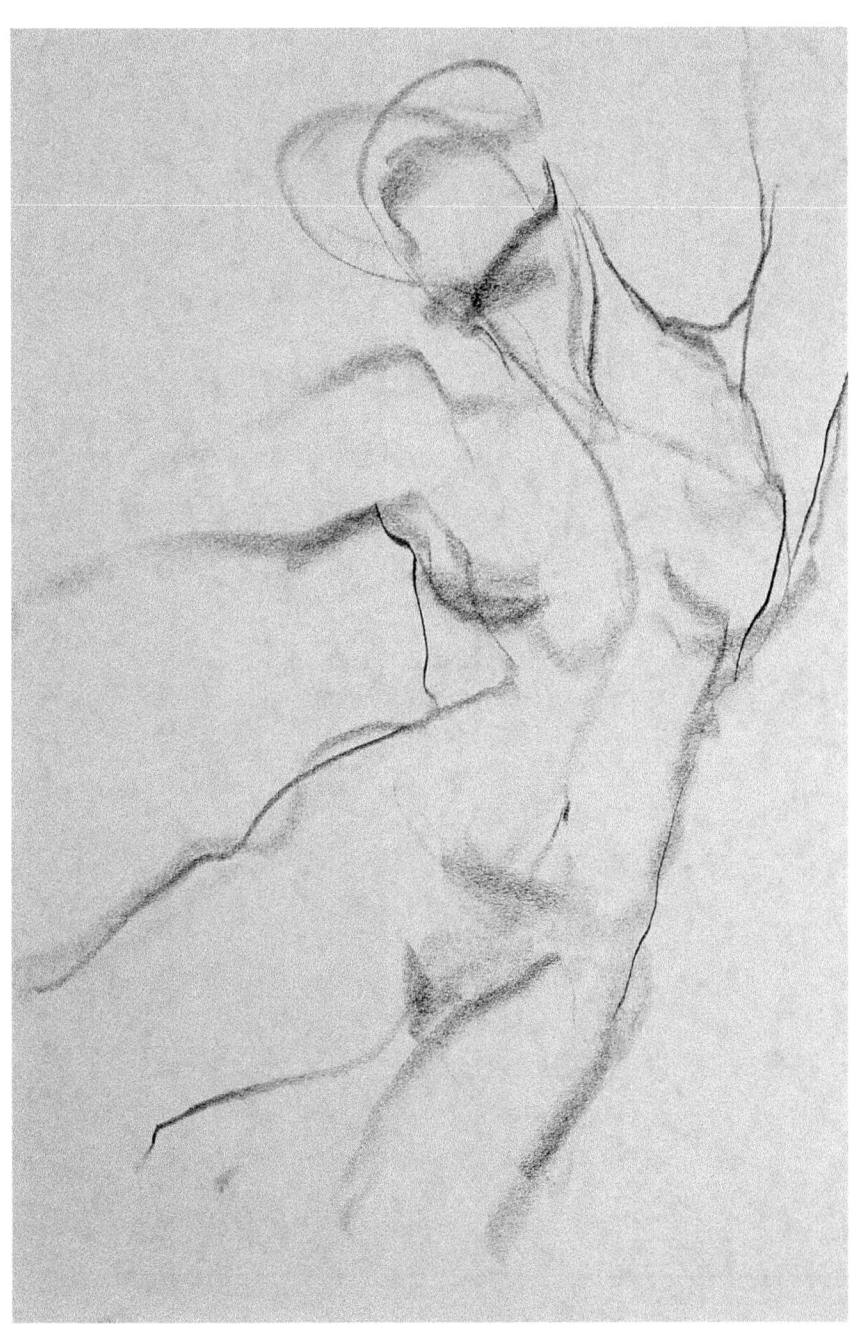

To Bend
1-2 Minute Drawing

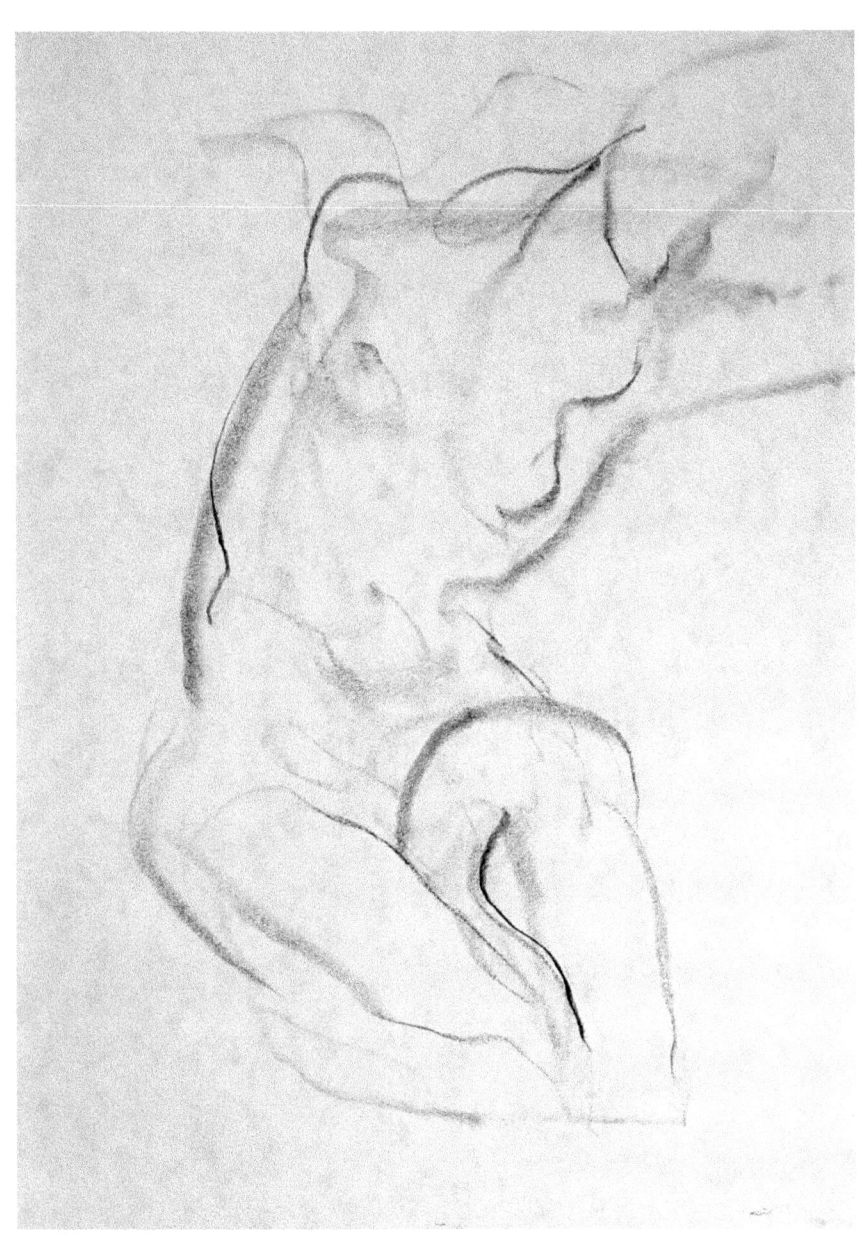

To Stretch
1-2 Minute Drawing

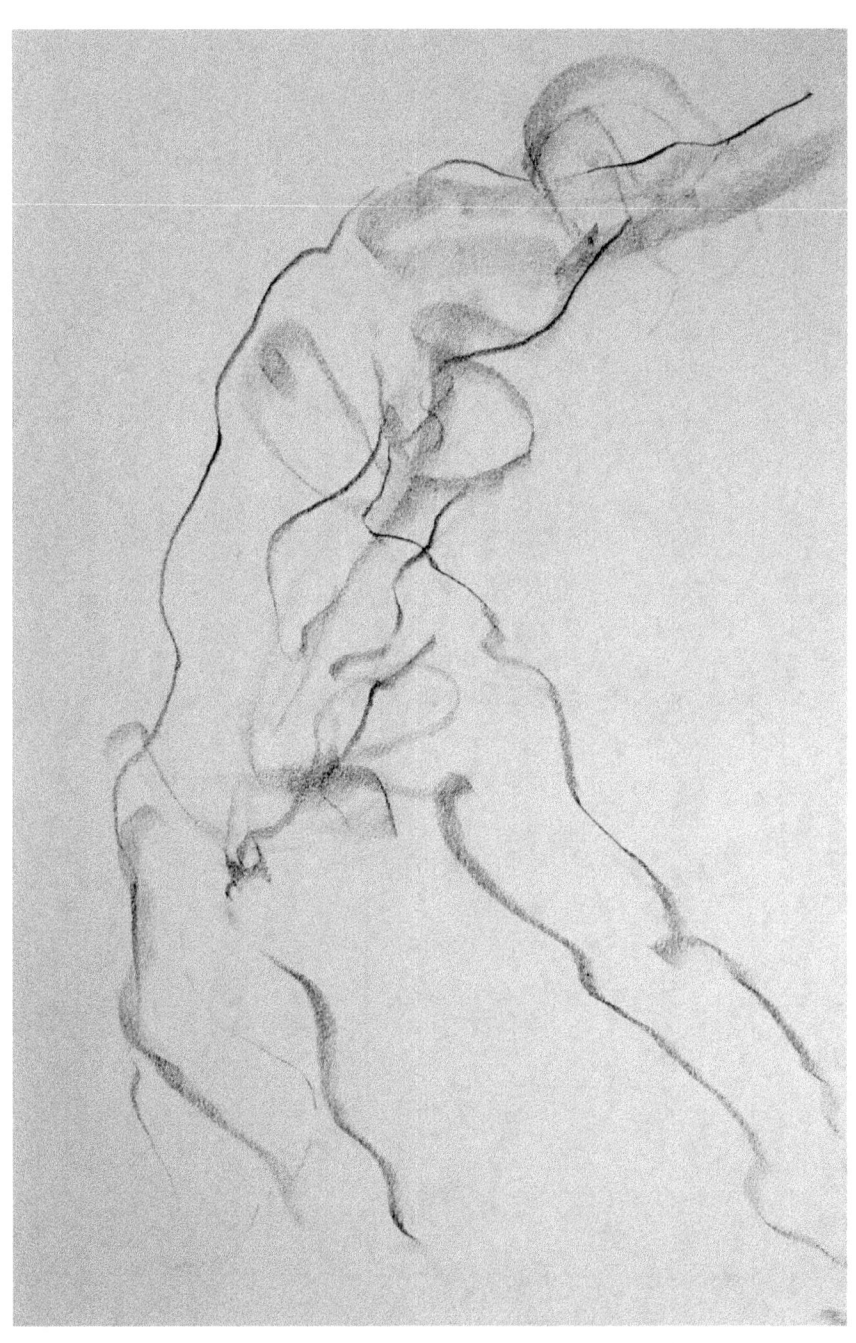

To Freeze
1-2 Minute Drawing

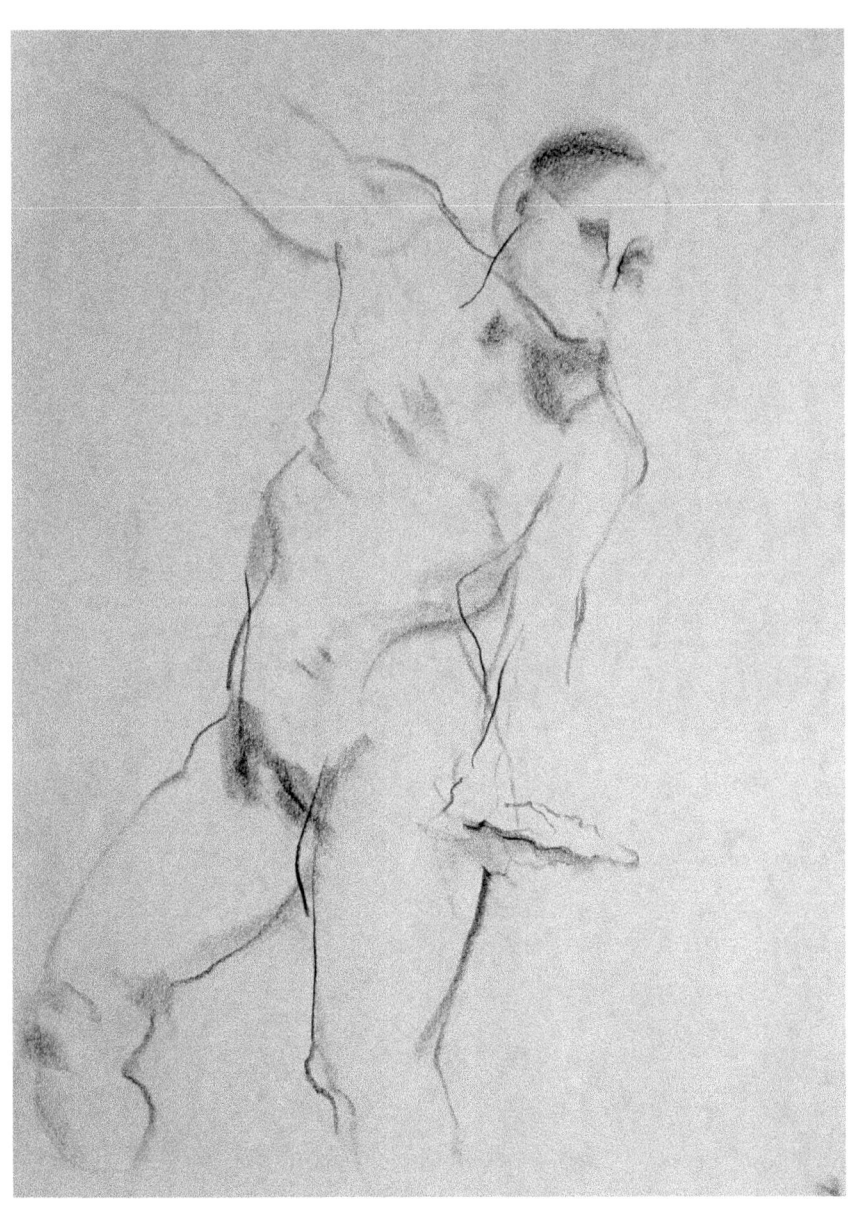

To Shift
1-2 Minute Drawing

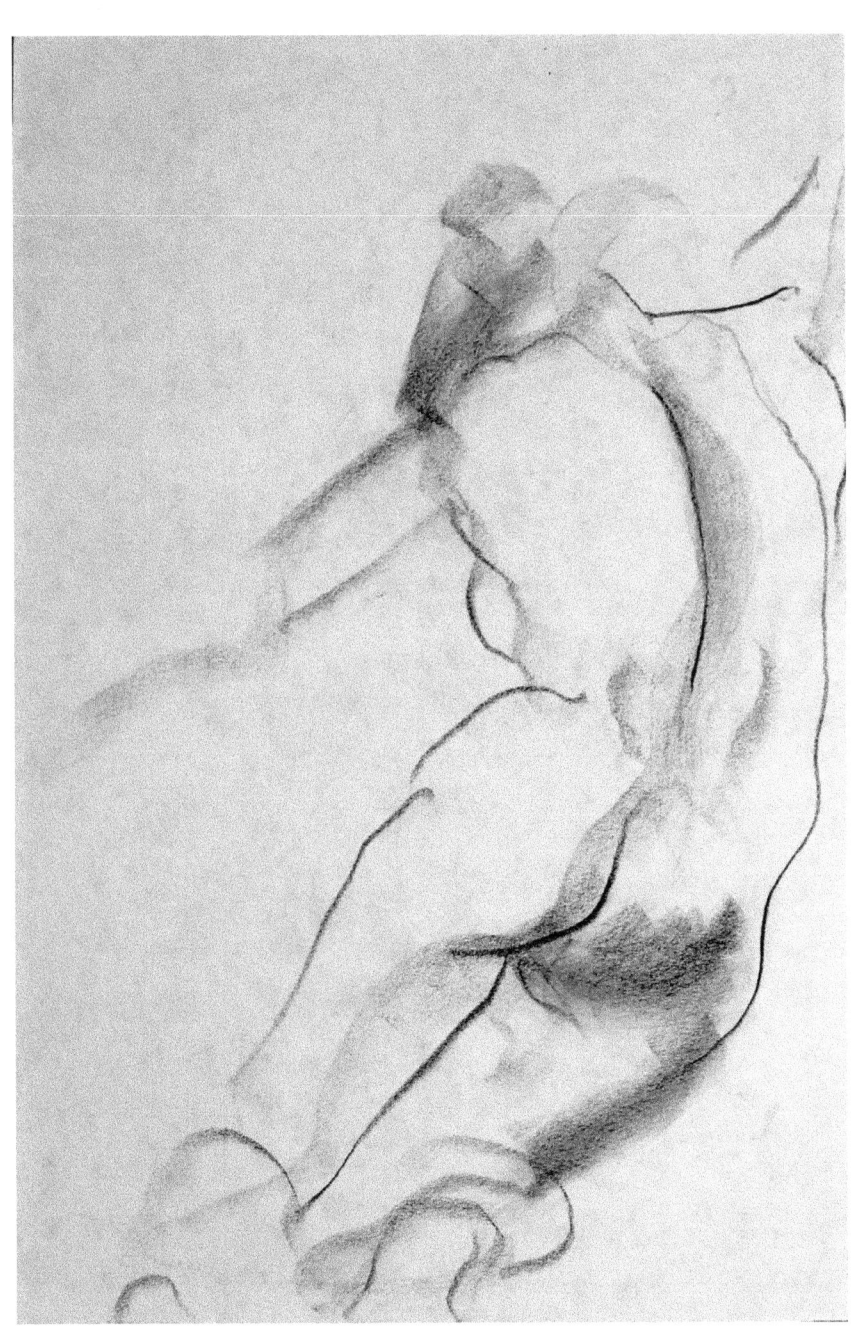

47

To Release
1-2 Minute Drawing

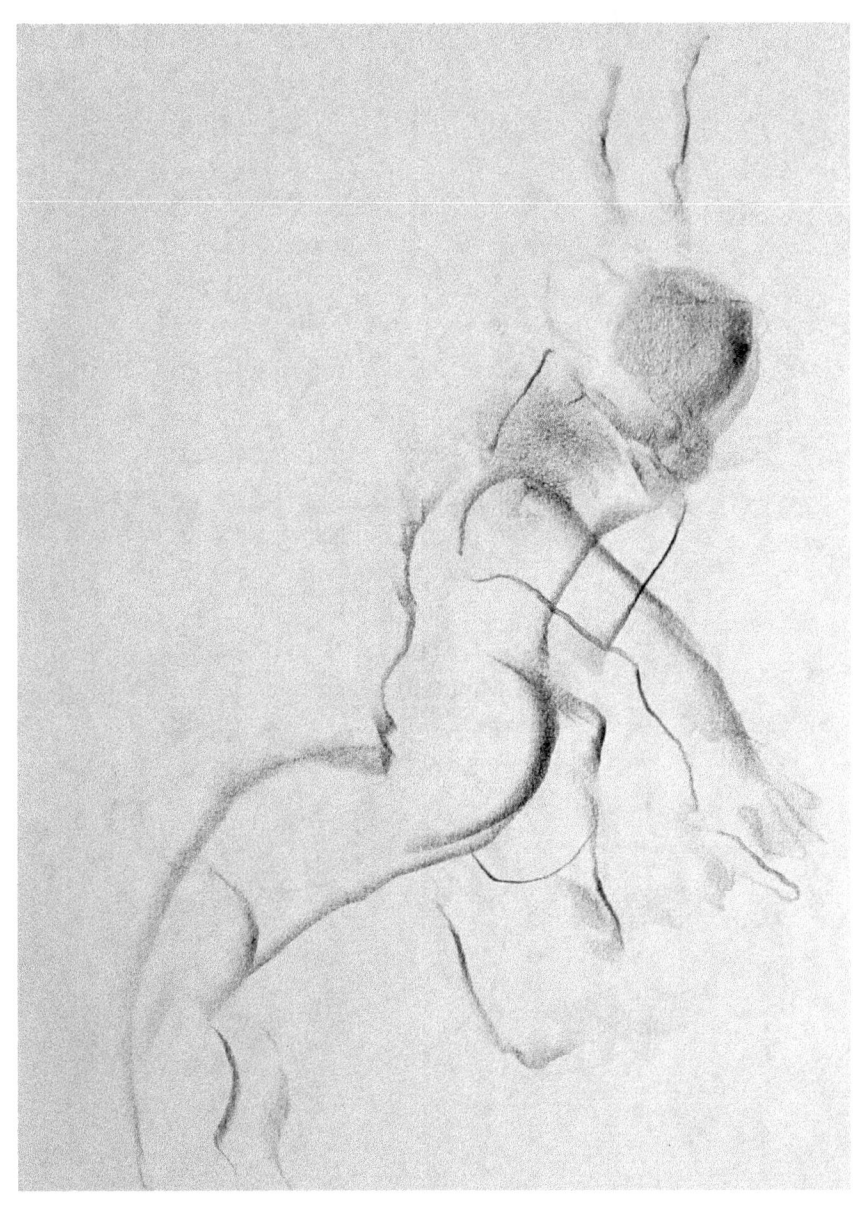

To Turn
1-2 Minute Drawing

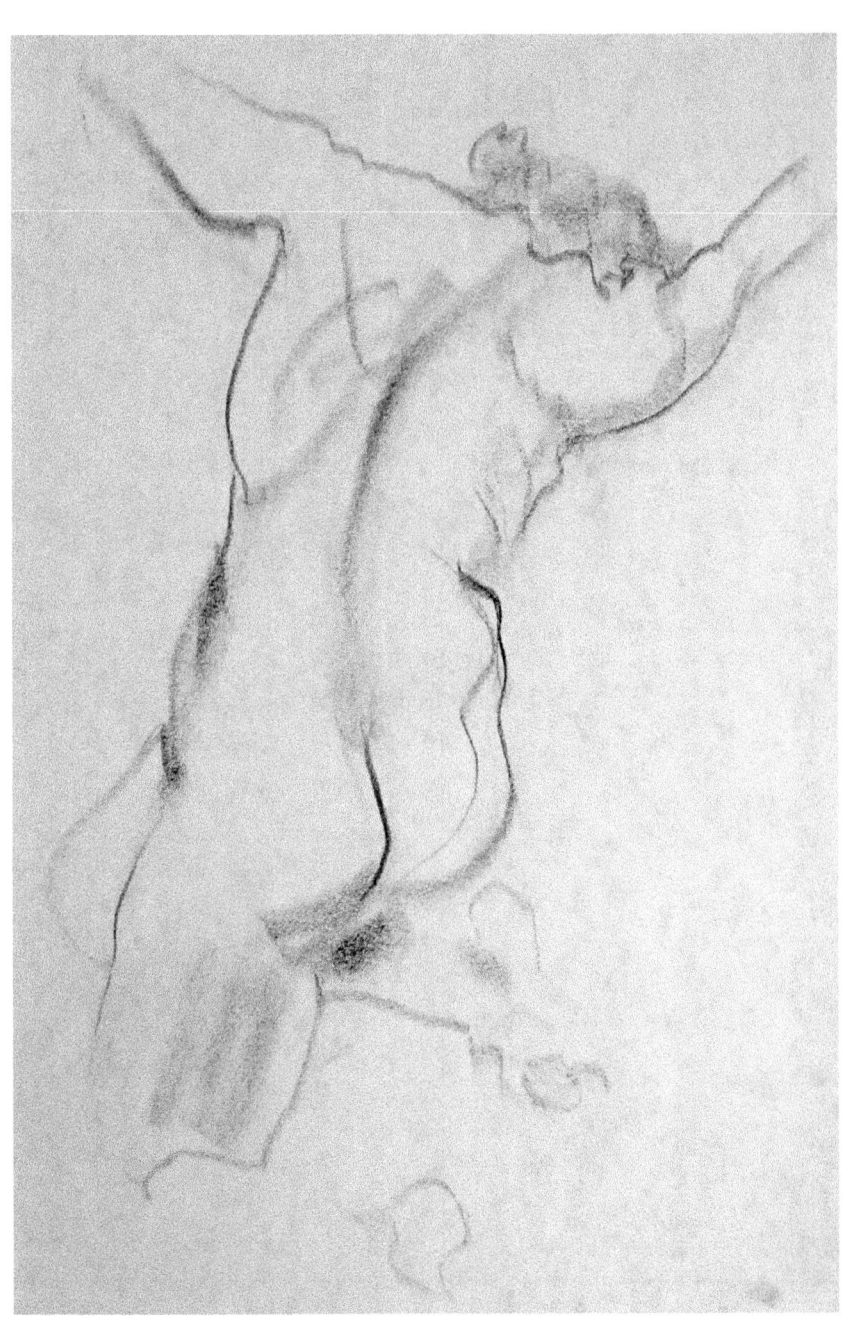

To Shrink
1-2 Minute Drawing

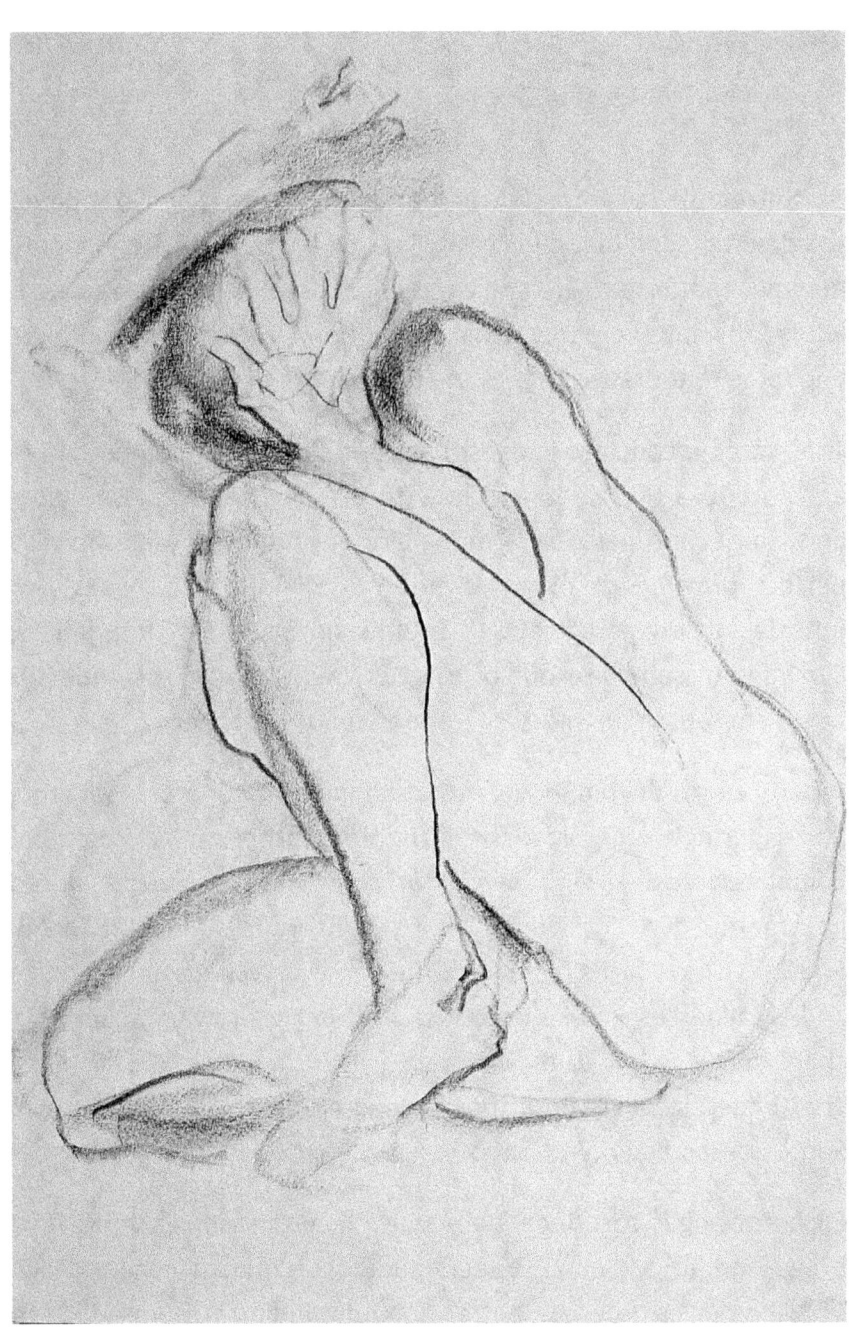

Twenty Minute Poses

To convey the livingness of the human figure on a piece of paper is a daunting and humbling task. To even try to capture the innate qualities that inspire life and express soul seems presumptuous. It exacts absolute empathy, total absorption, entire absence of ego. The force that draws me in is so compelling—I surrender—I try.

There are no concrete images that define abstract qualities. There are no books that show me how to draw what I can't see. Soul and spirit are palpable, intangible, mysterious. A technically perfect drawing of either is beyond my physical senses and outside of my imagination. Soulful qualities are fathomless. Qualities of spirit are out of reach. When my ego surrenders—when I'm rapt in the mystery—understanding happens.

When I begin drawing I know that soon self-awareness will fade. Surrendering to the process I drop into another realm. When I'm completely lost—I find myself *in the zone*. Previously stored information surfaces. I draw until self-awareness looms its head. Pausing, I have a dialogue with the drawing—check its strengths and weaknesses—make decisions, and begin drawing again. In a short time *I'm lost in the process—I'm in the zone—I'm in bliss*. The process repeats until the drawing assumes a life of its own. Some do—some don't.

Each drawing is part of an ever-evolving continuum. Each drawing brings me to a clearer understanding of human nature. Each drawing gives me a better understanding of myself. To understand more is the lure that draws me in. I know where I've been, but I don't know where I'm going. If I knew there would be no intrigue—no mystery to unveil. It's about answering those gnawing questions, "Who am I?" "Why am I here?"

Gertrude Stein wrote, *A rose is a rose is a rose.* The more I see into my own nature, the more transparent all nature becomes. My attempt to touch both spirit and soul is an act of love. Love is the attraction. Love is the desire, the urgency, the impelling force that prods me to wake up to the wonder of human nature. *Love is a universal drive—relentless—all inclusive—unconditional.*

The Past is Present

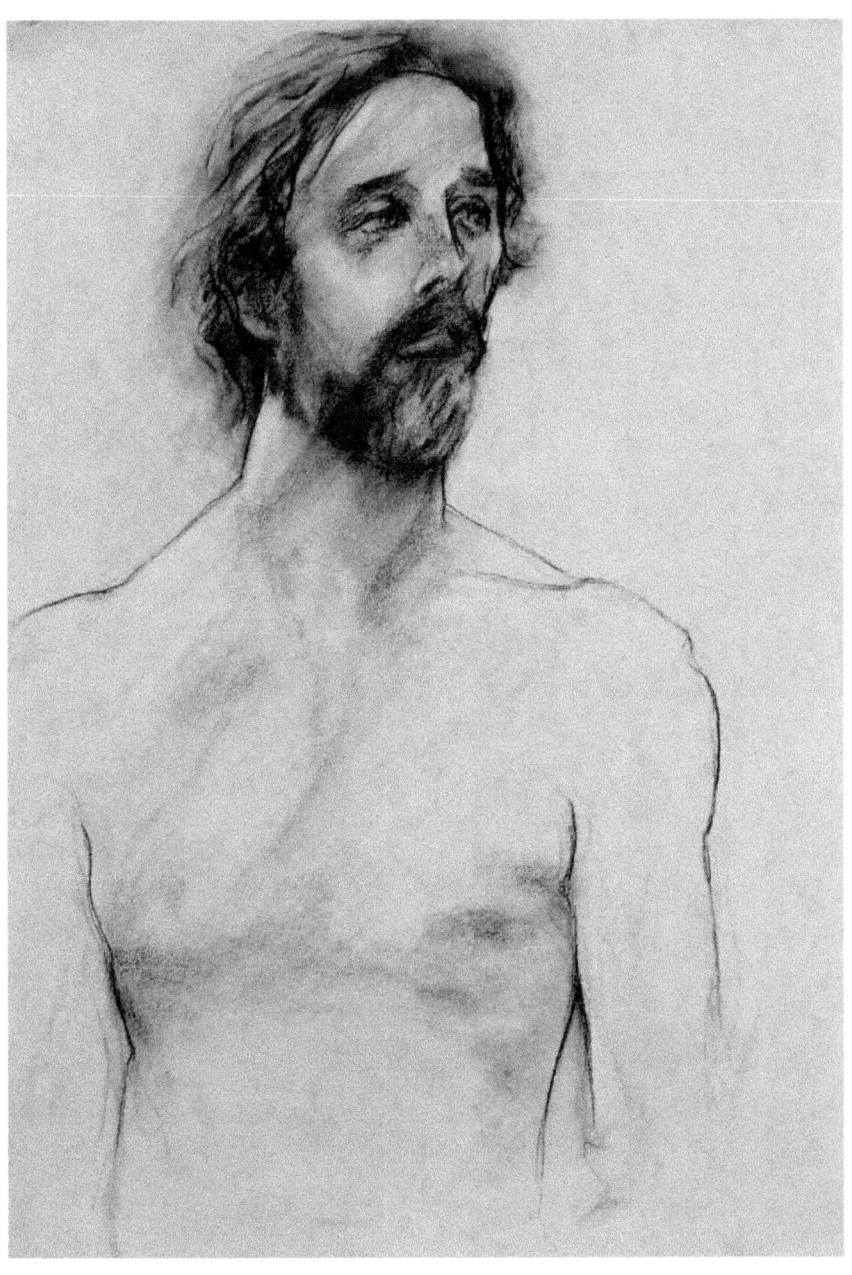

All Possibilities

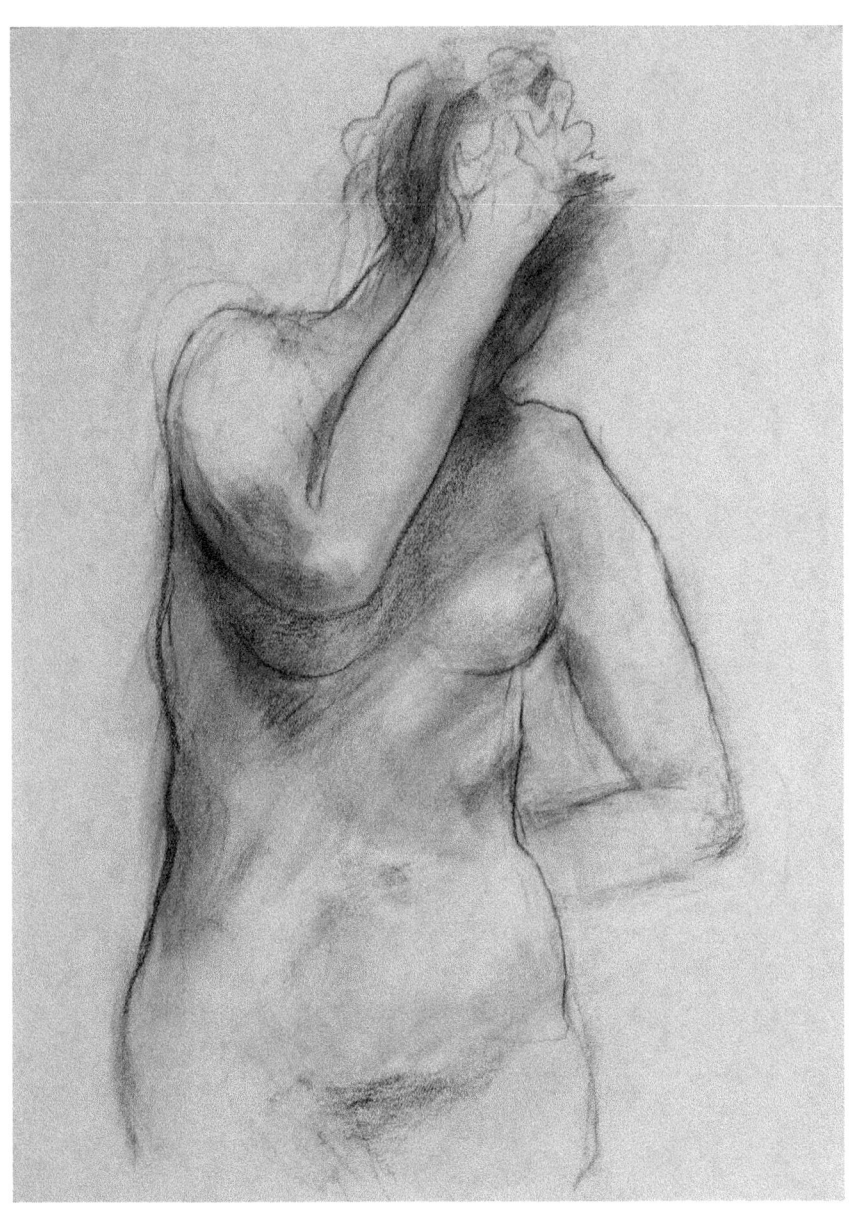

Holding Place

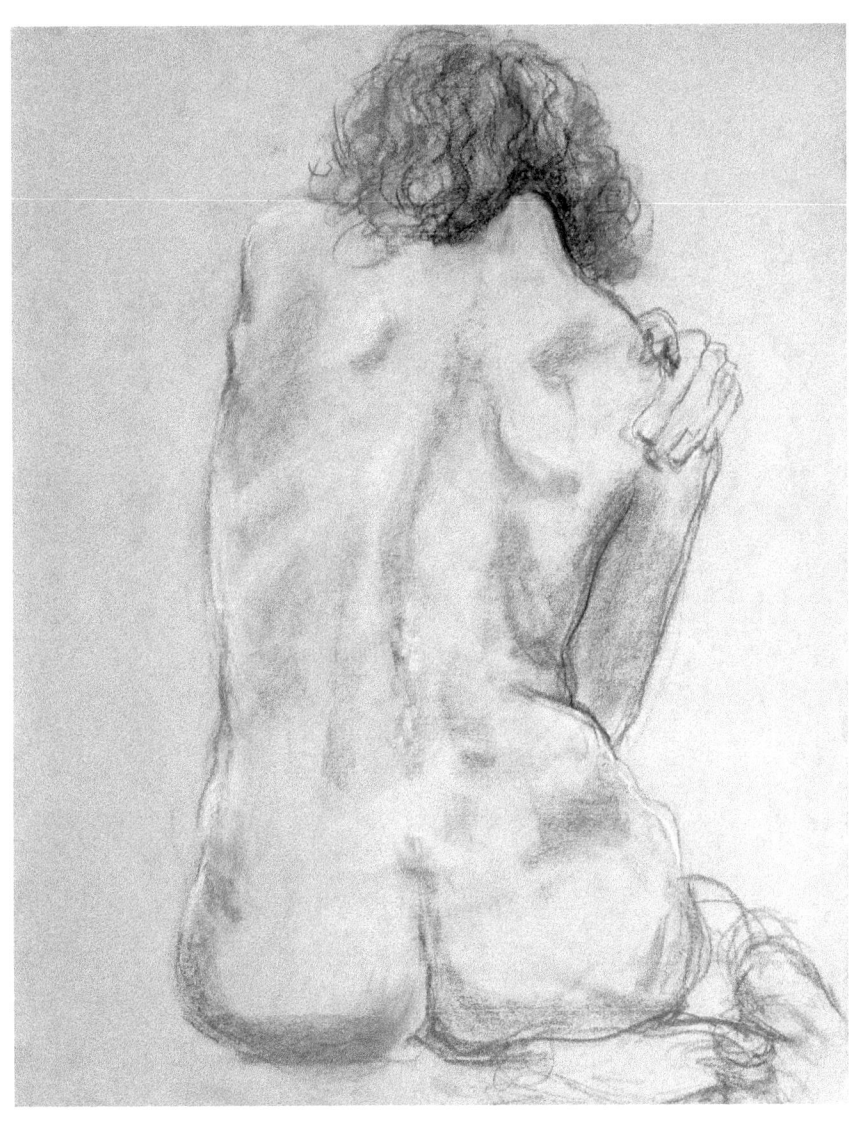

Love Can Be Tough

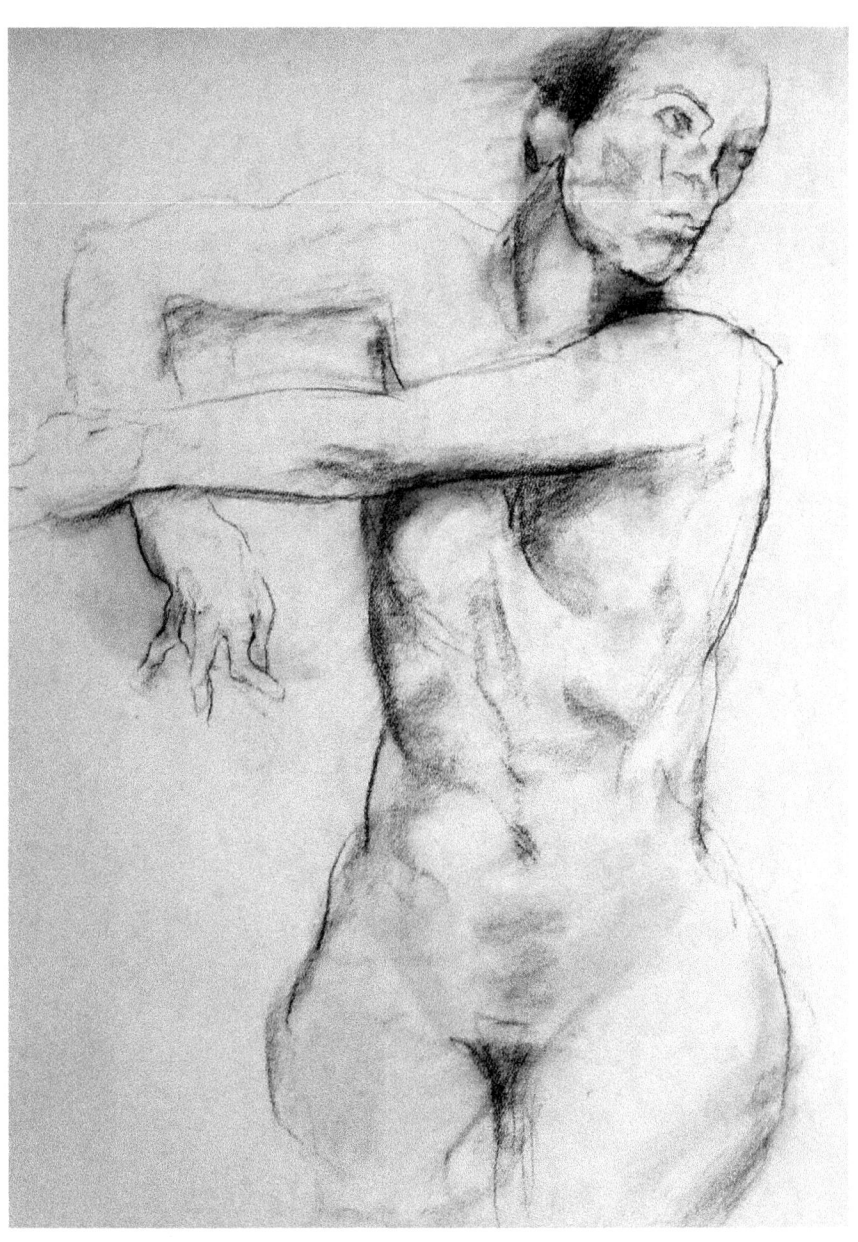

Soul Cries

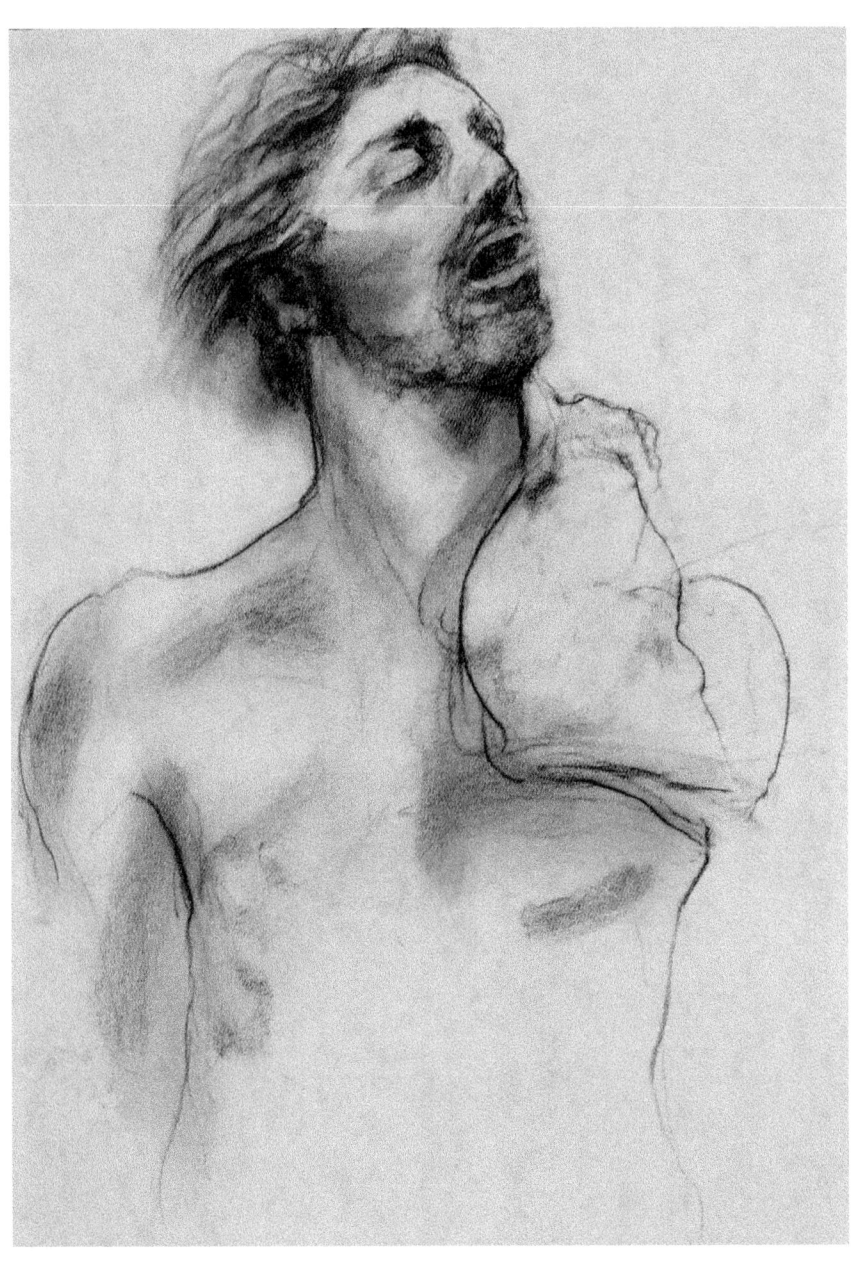

Looking Back

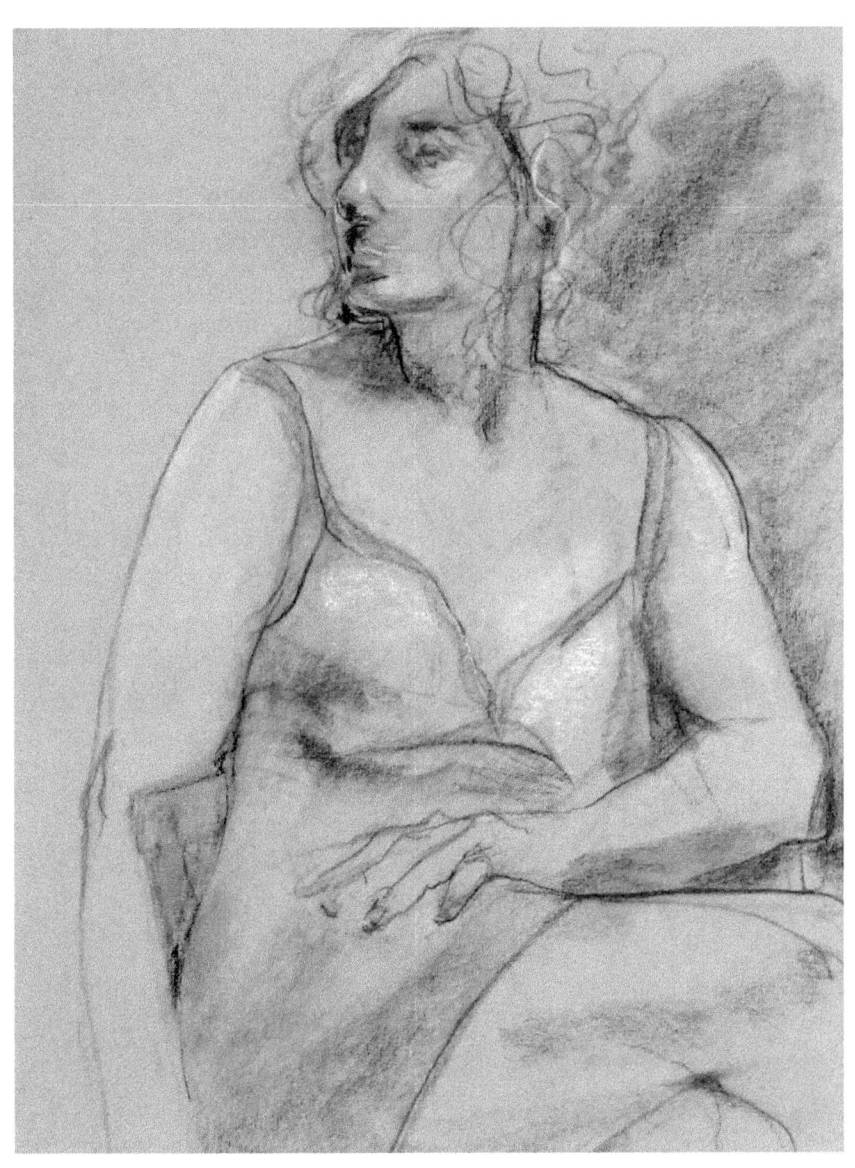

Rapt in Mystery

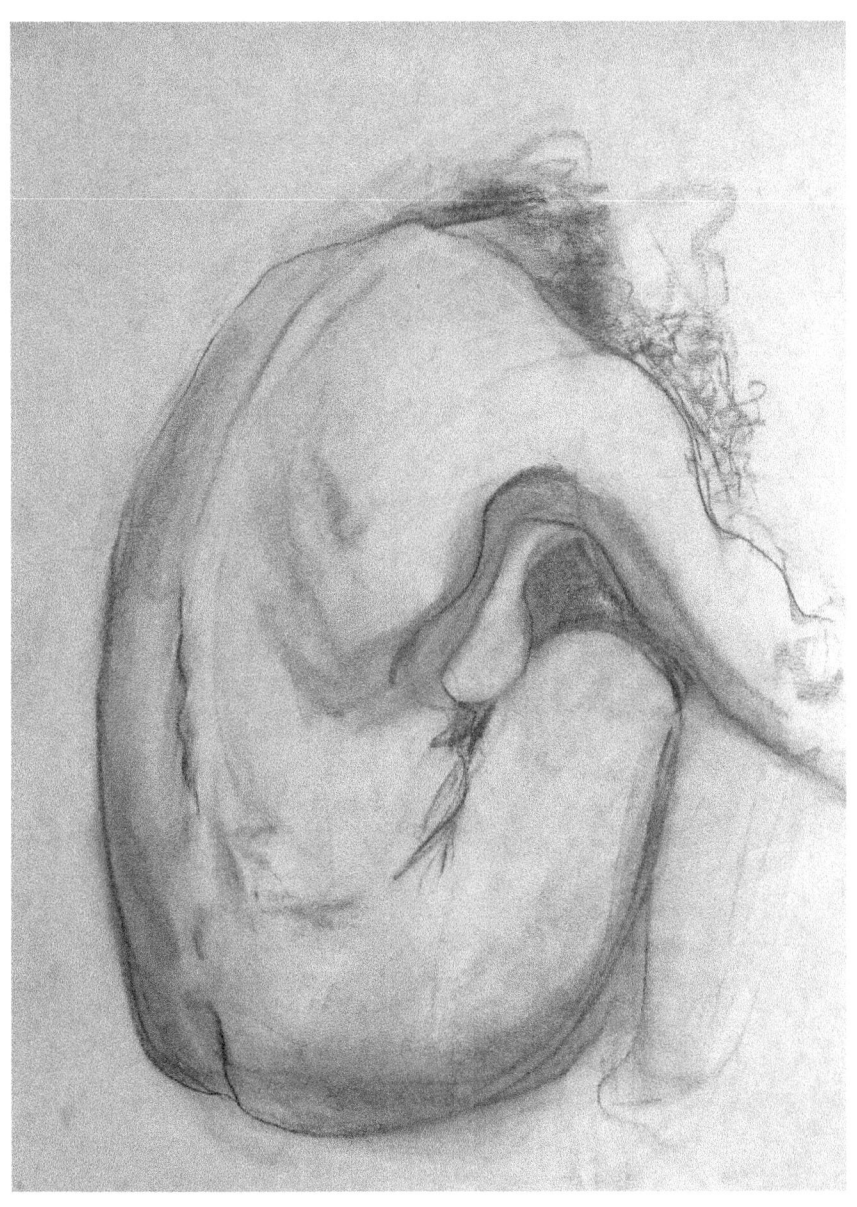

I've Changed Several Times
Since Morning

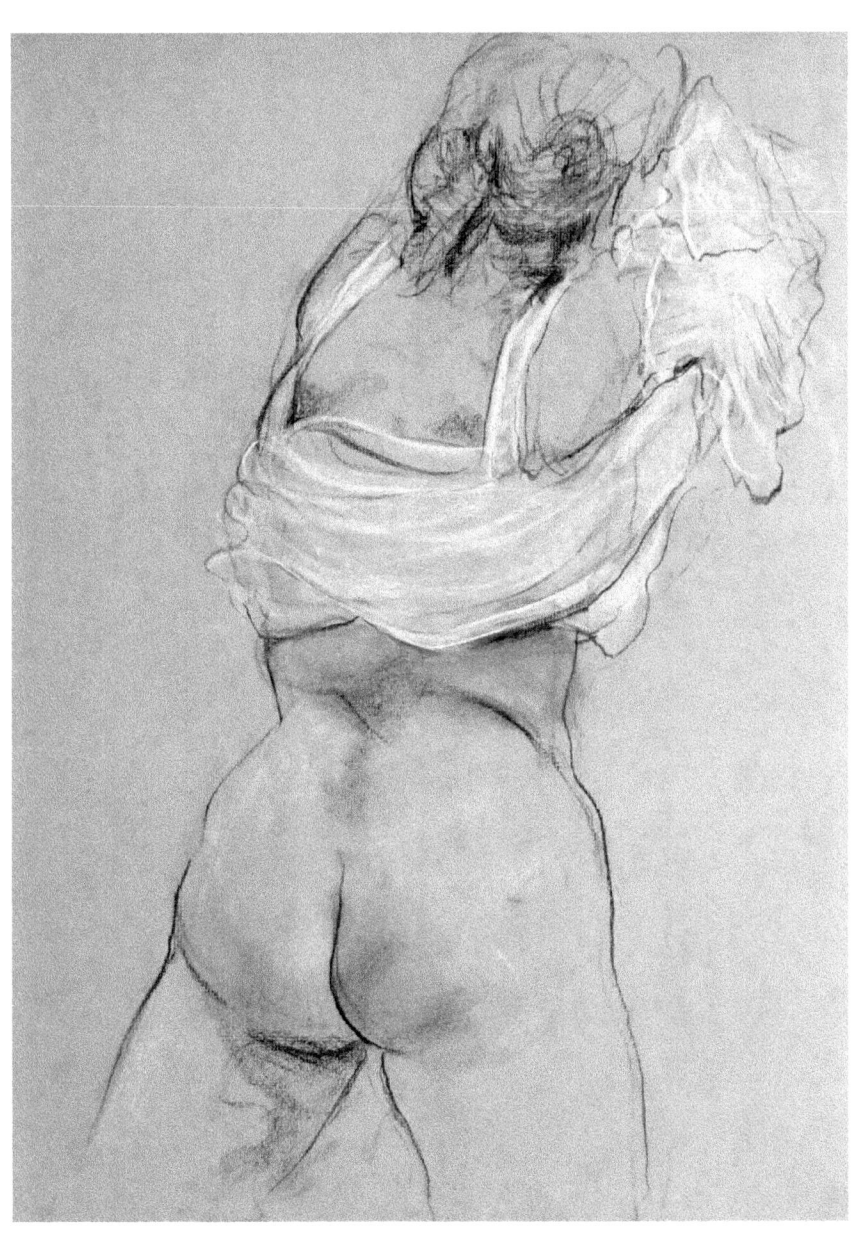

Lost in Memory

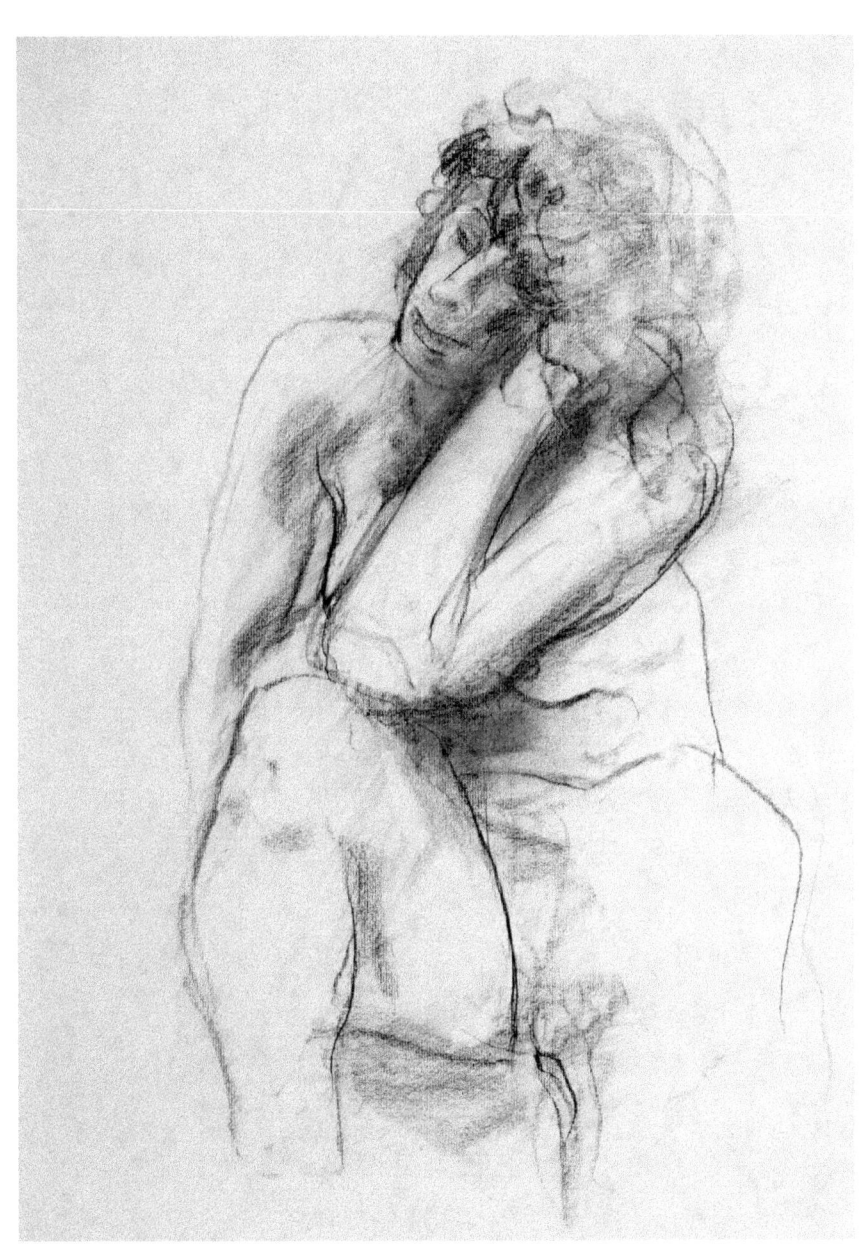

Struck by Lightning

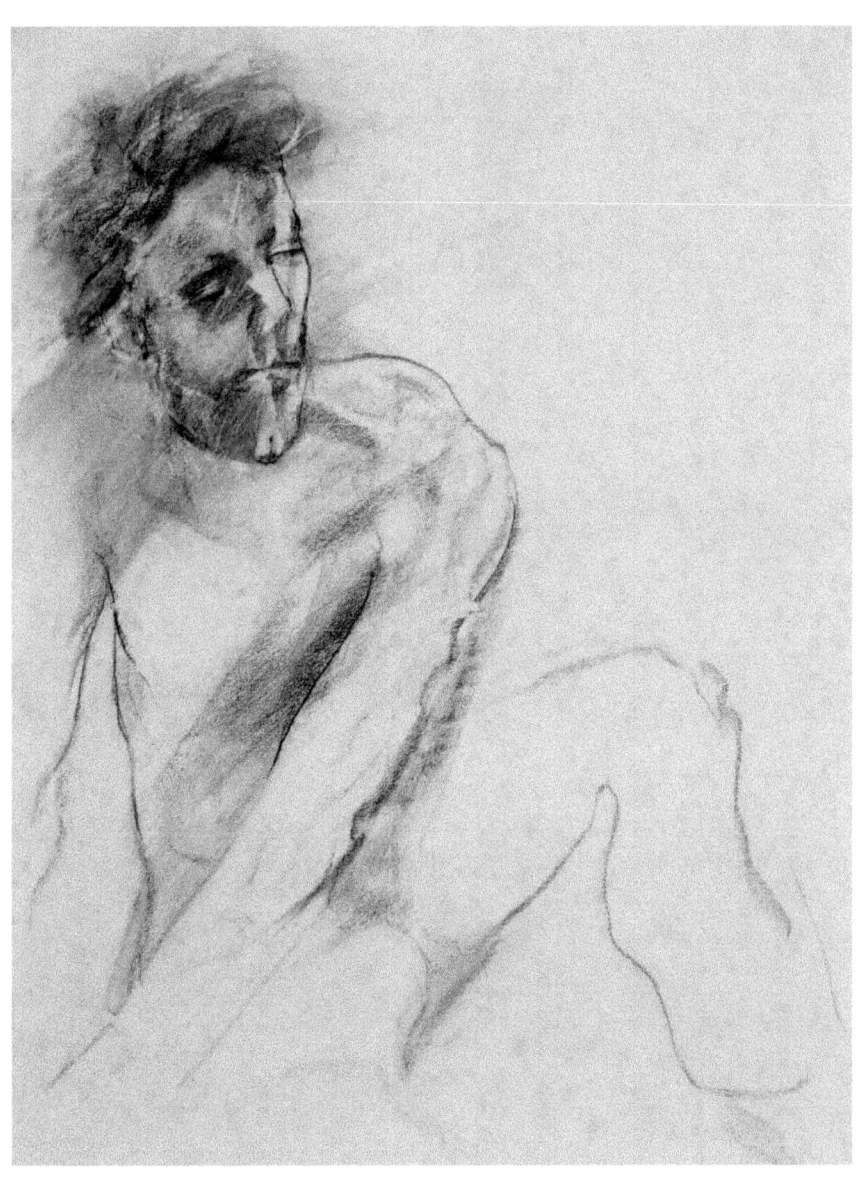

In the Dark

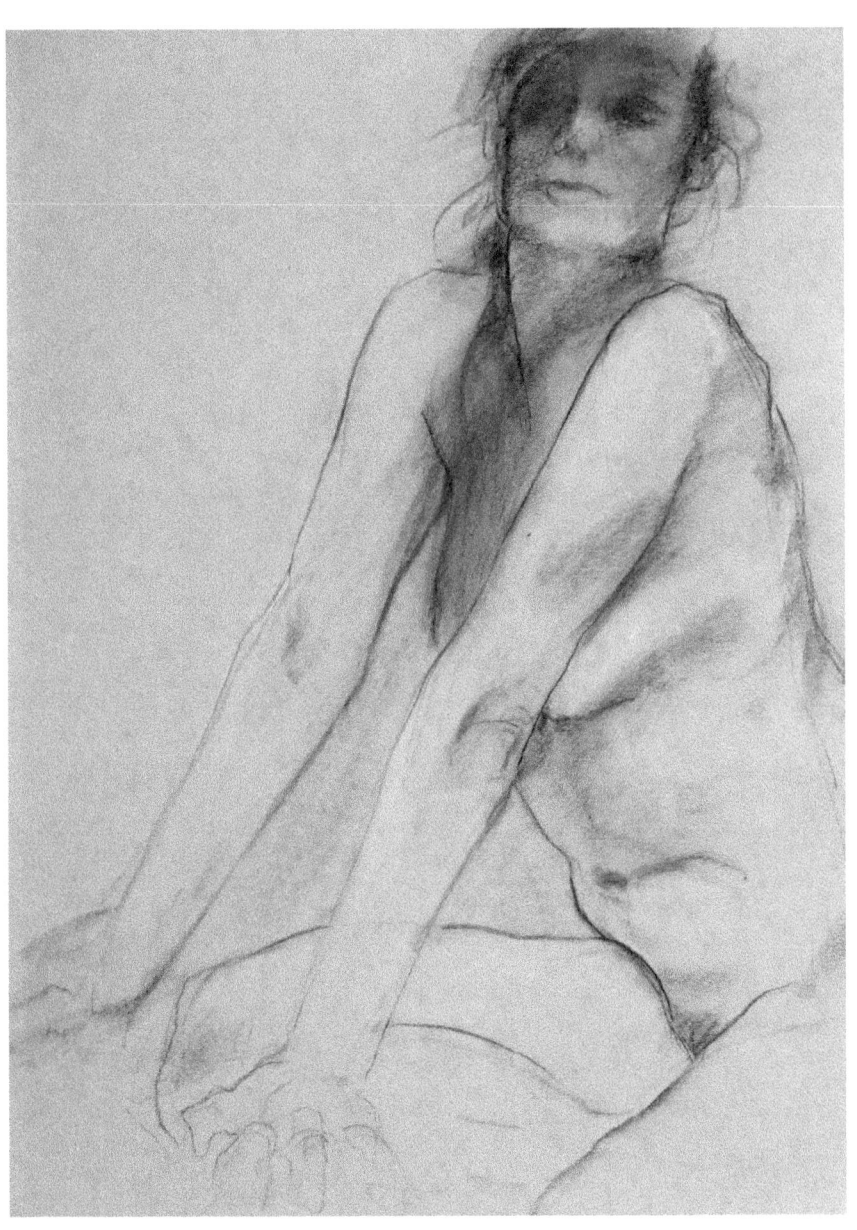

Inside of Love

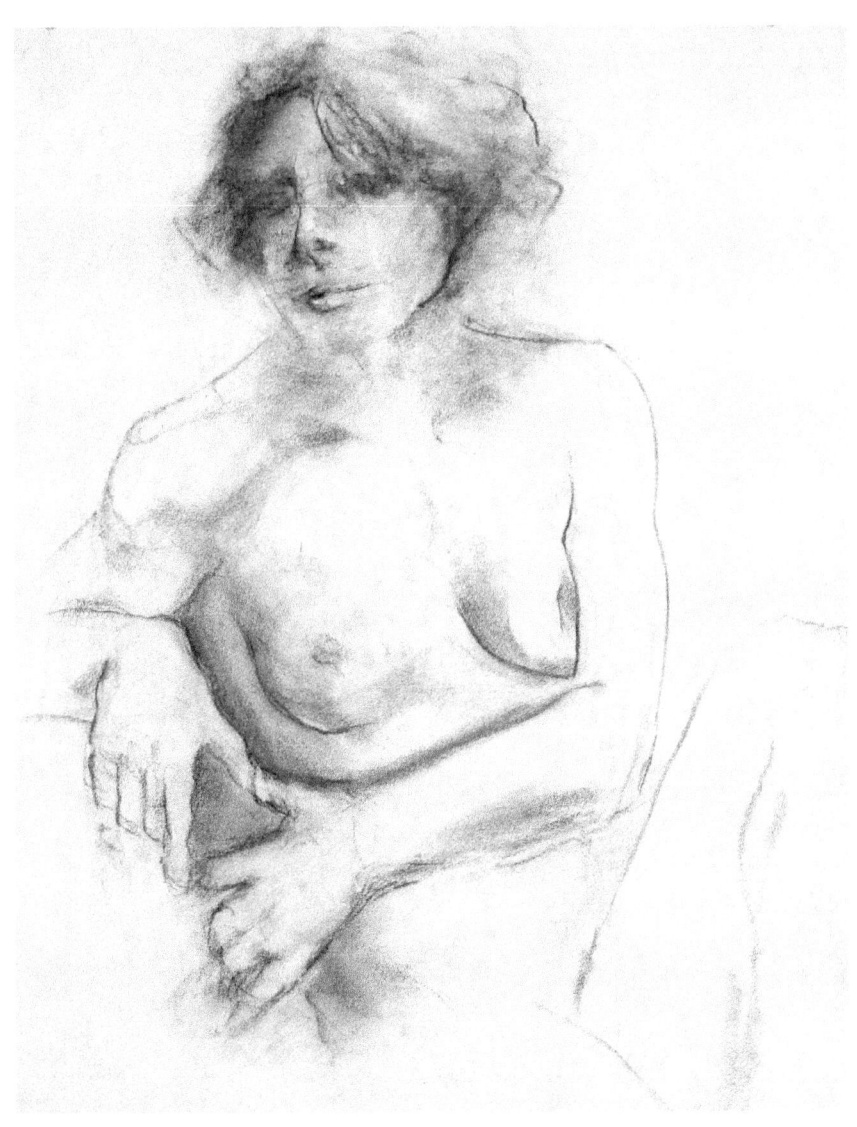

Triggered Fear

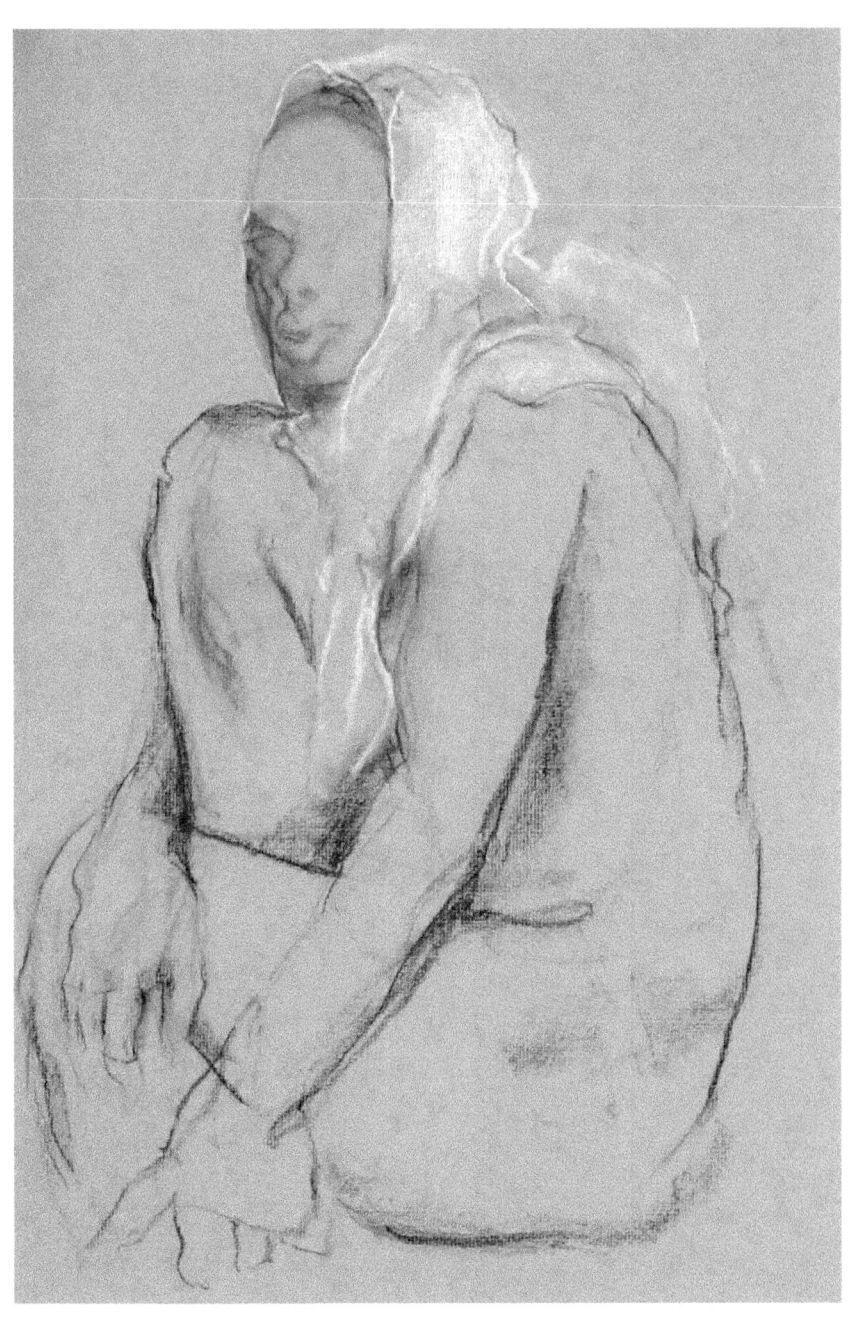

Embracing Change

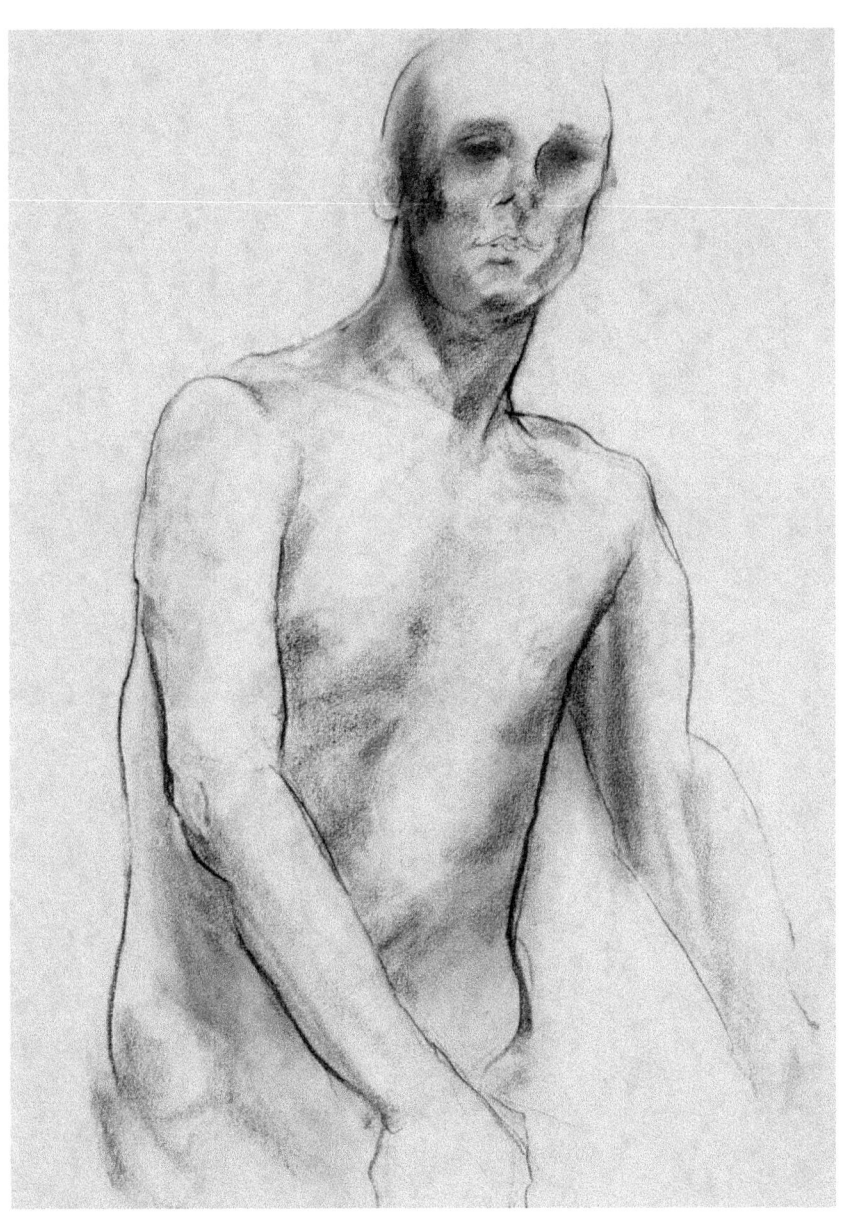

Letting Go

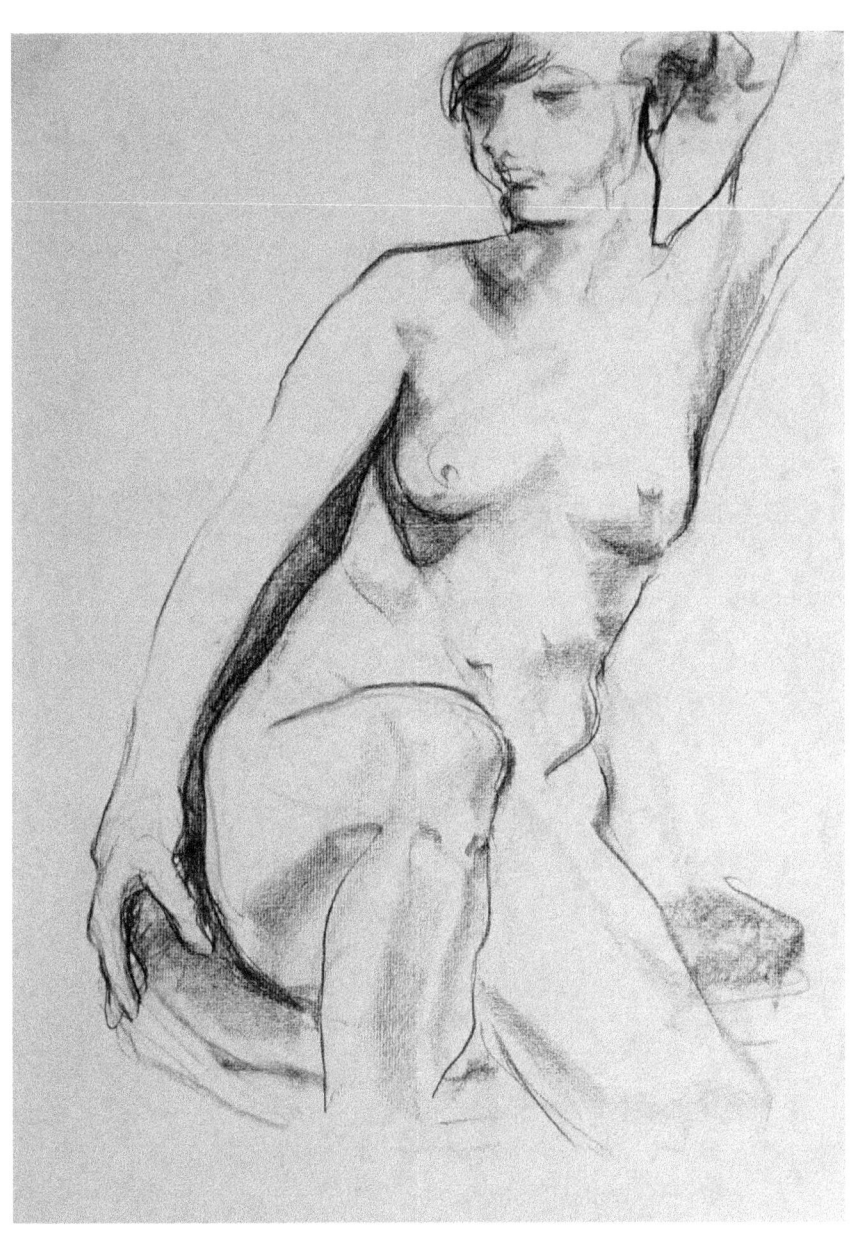

Dissolving Ego

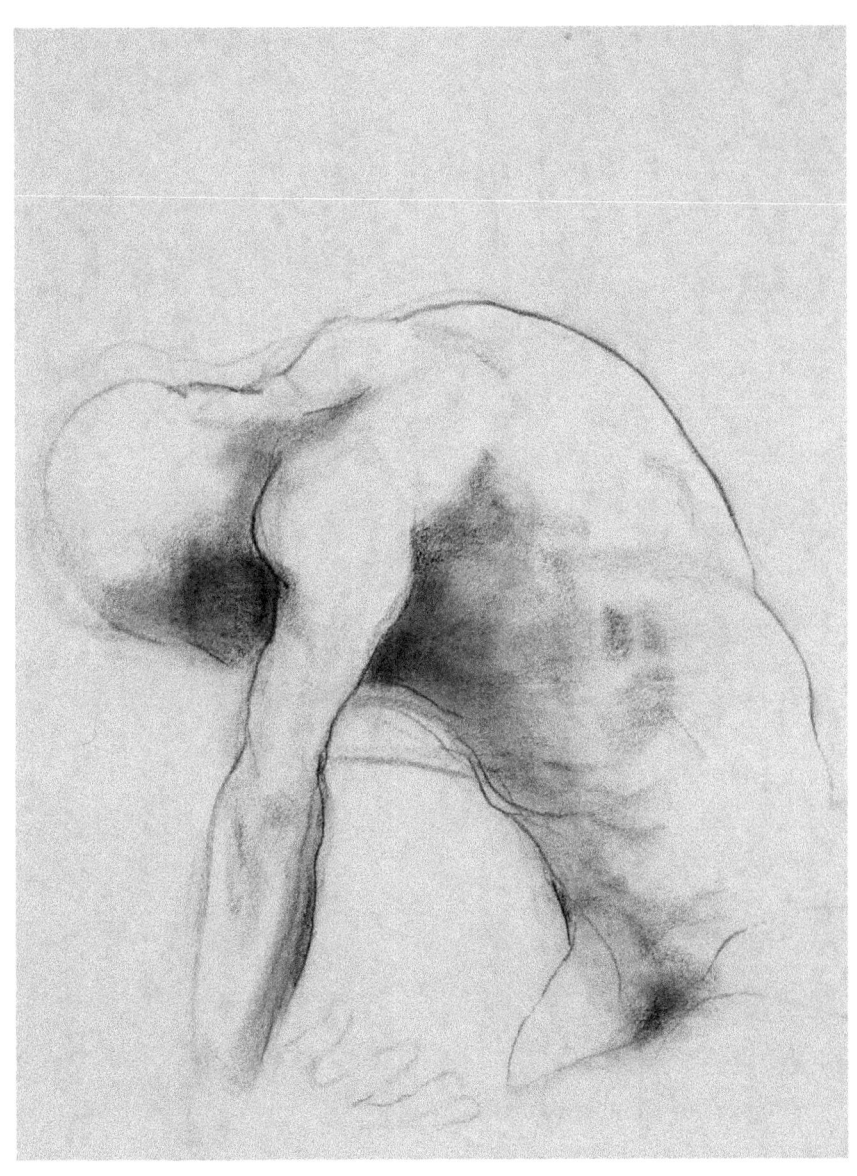

In Light of The Eye

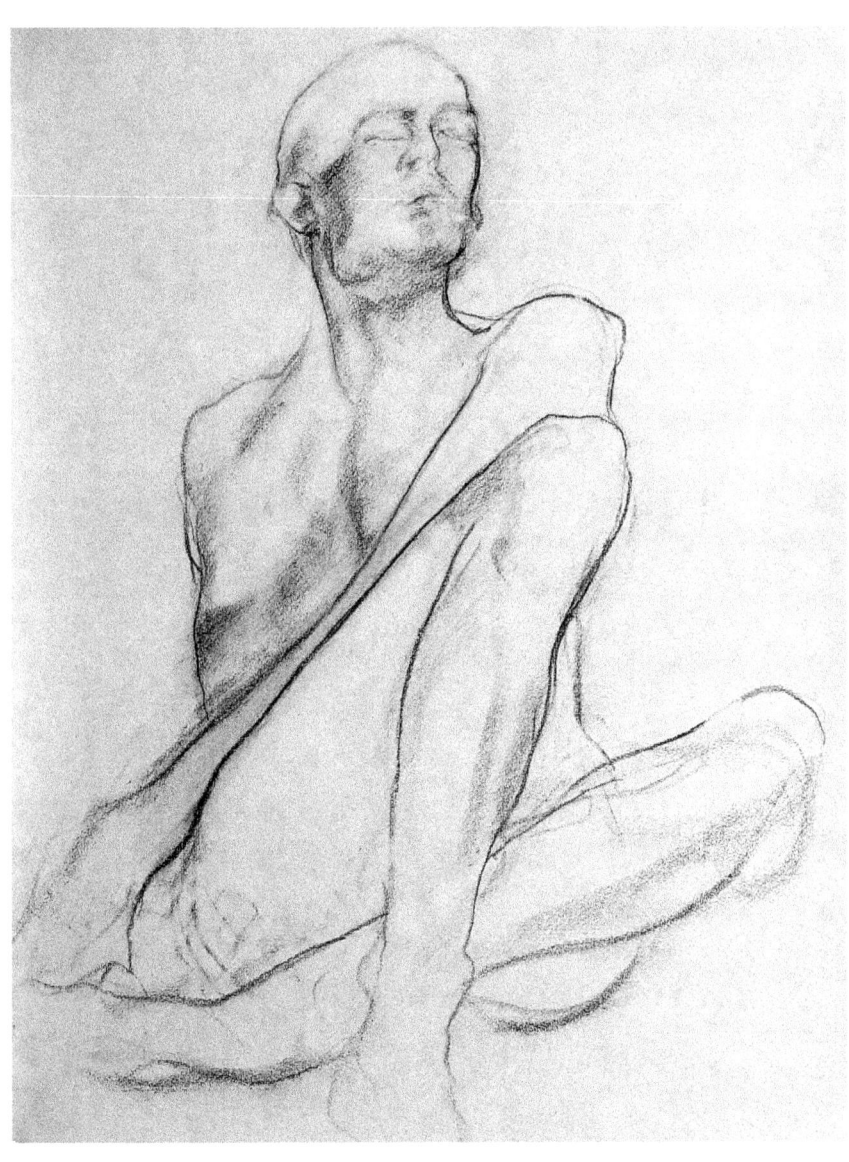

Reawakening

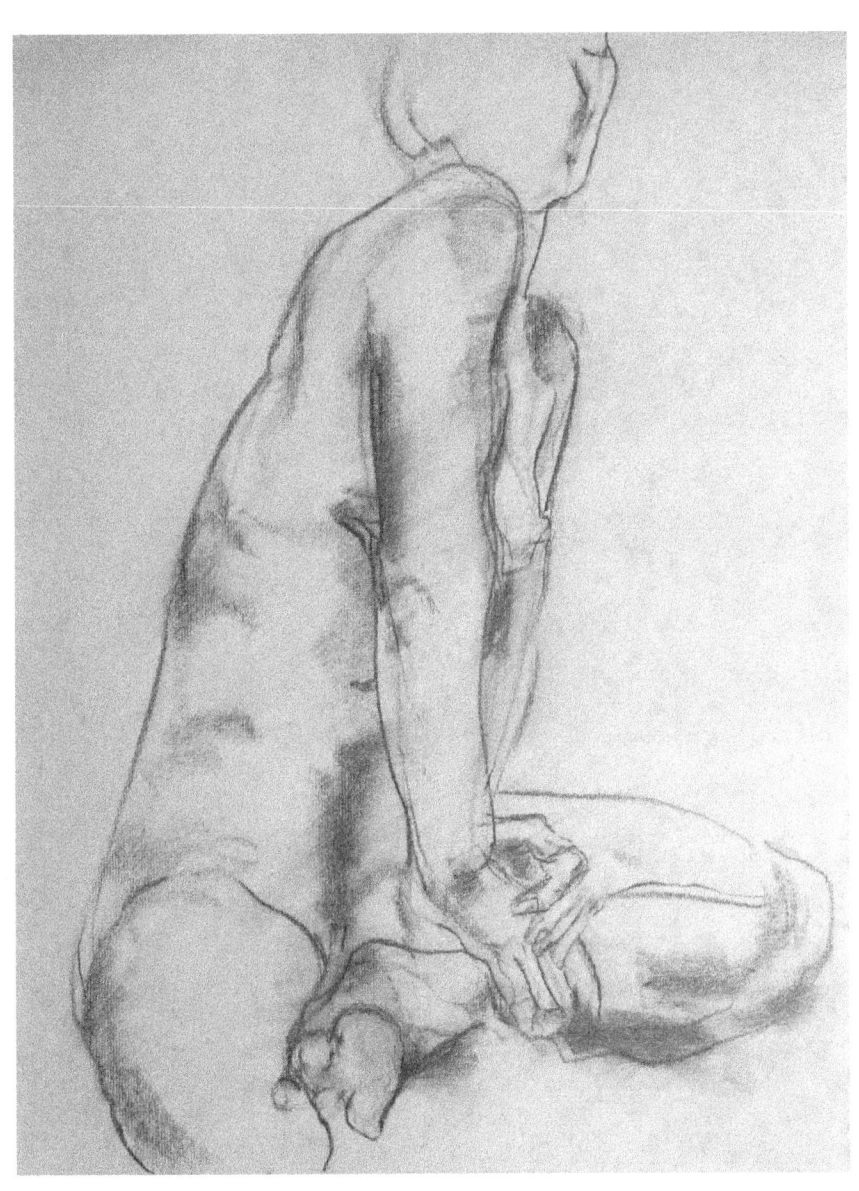

Soul Whispers

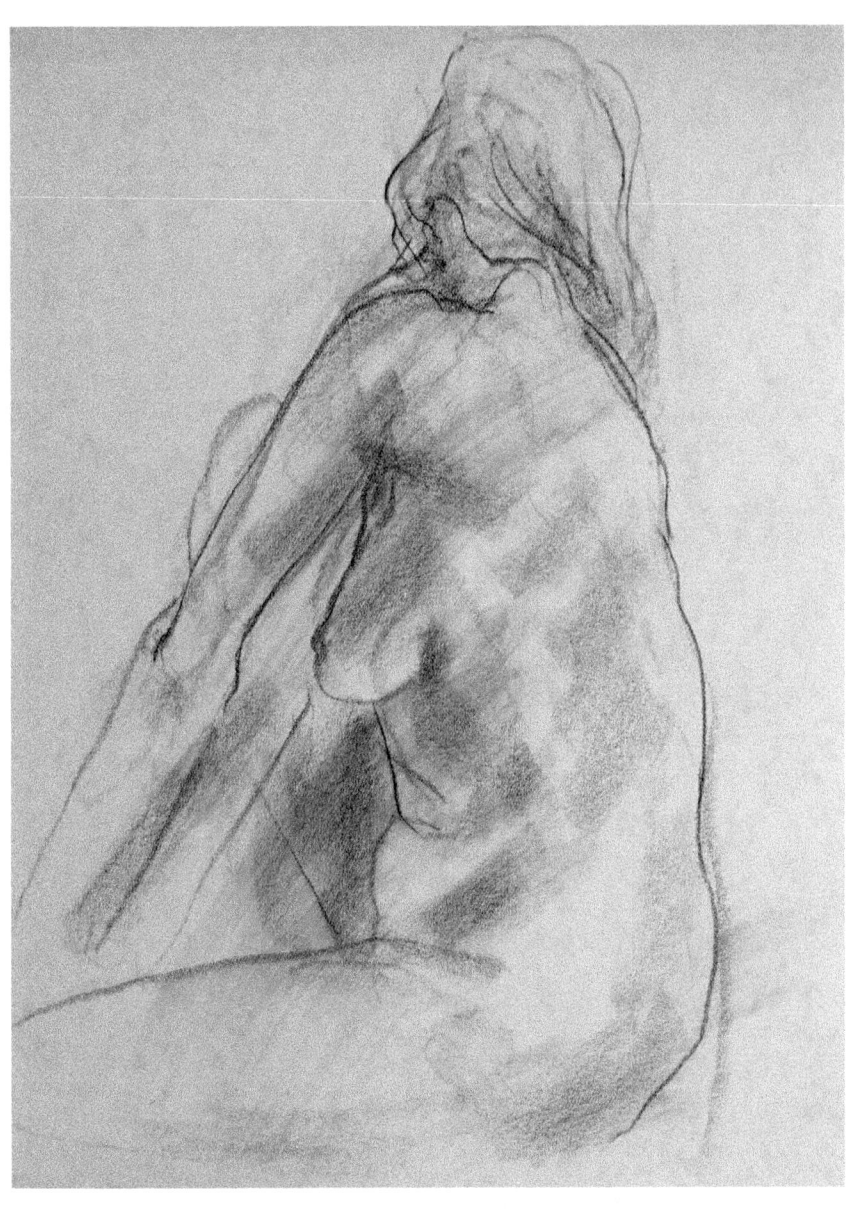

Unguarded—Ungrounded—Uncertain

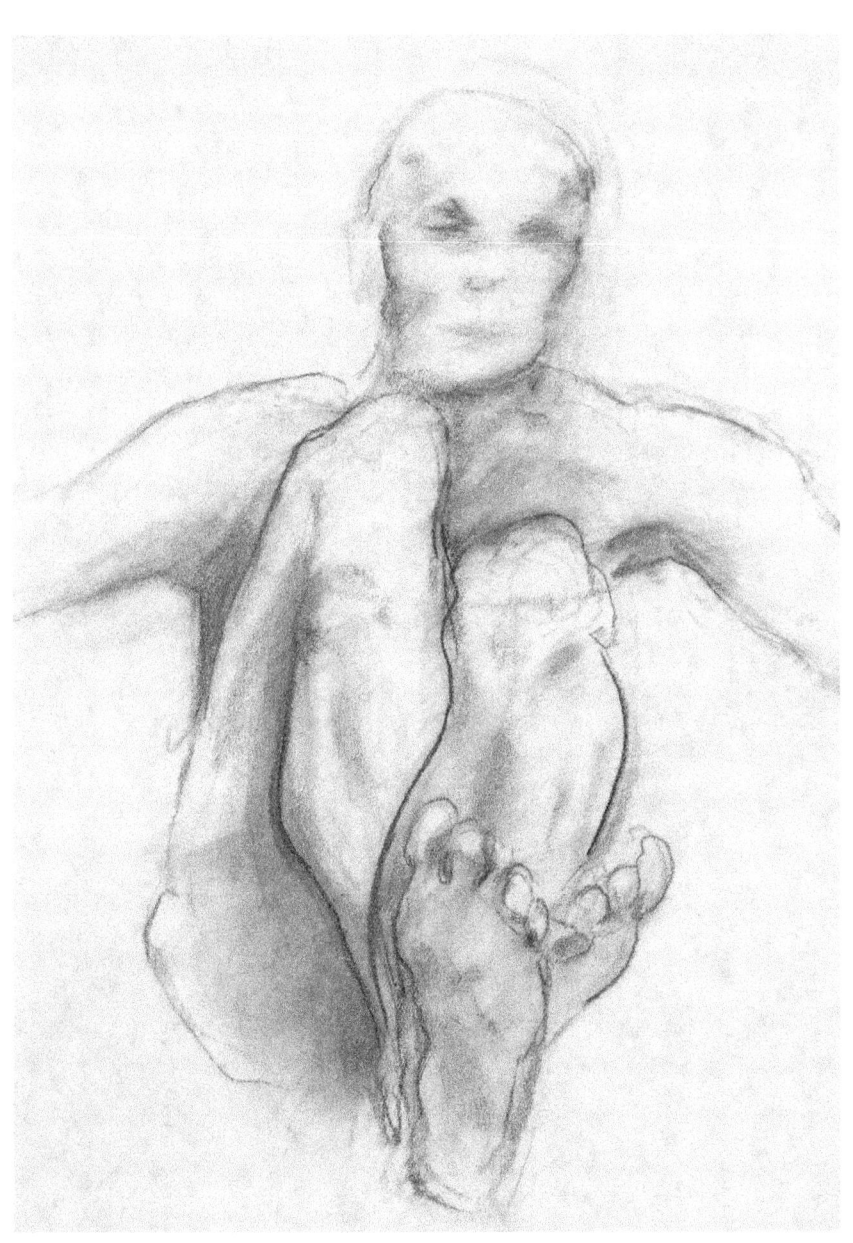

Seeing Another Perspective

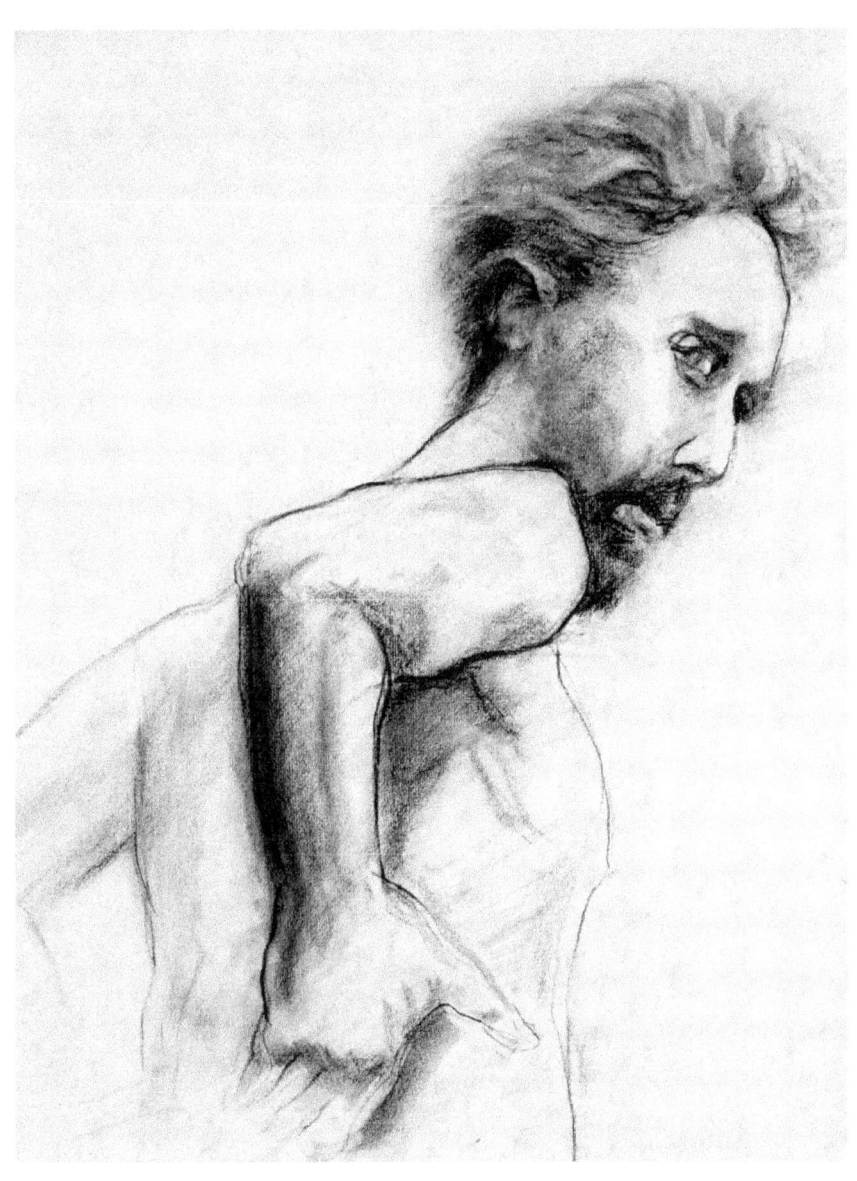

Indecision

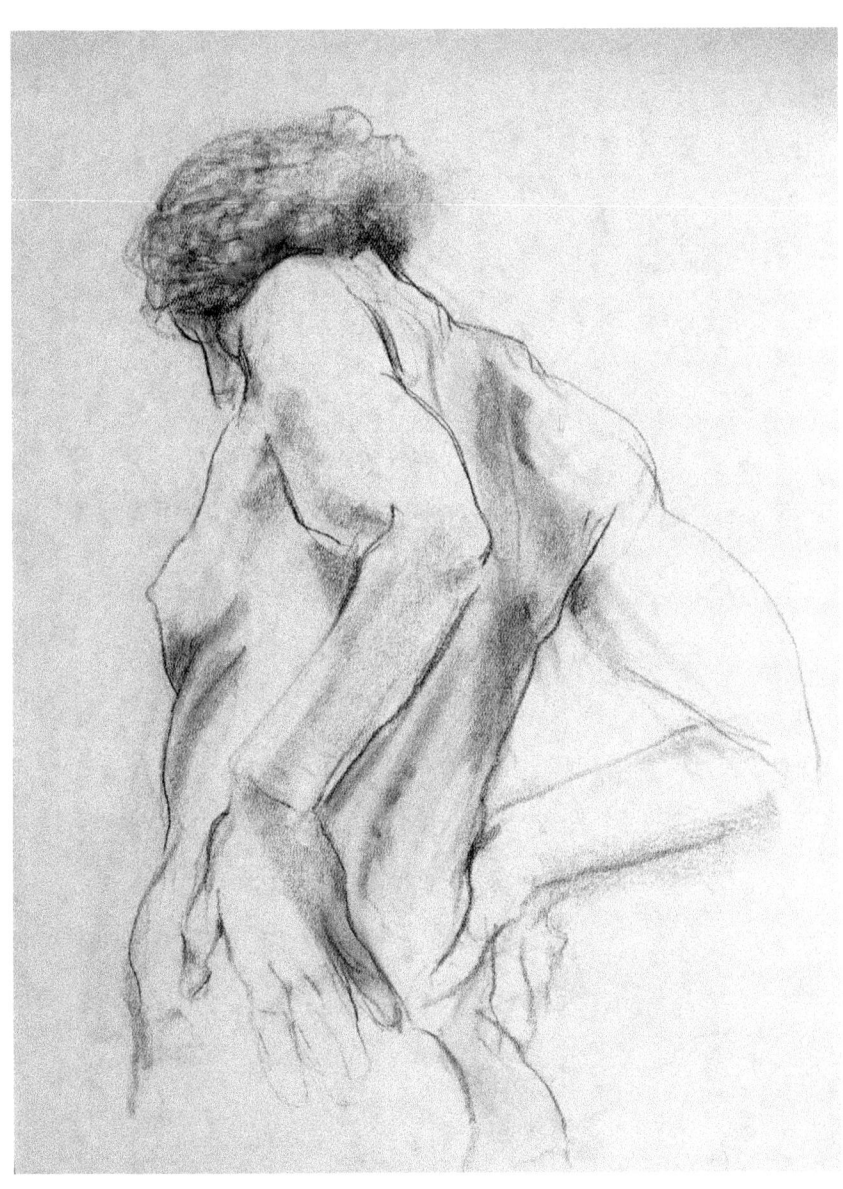

Reflections Surface

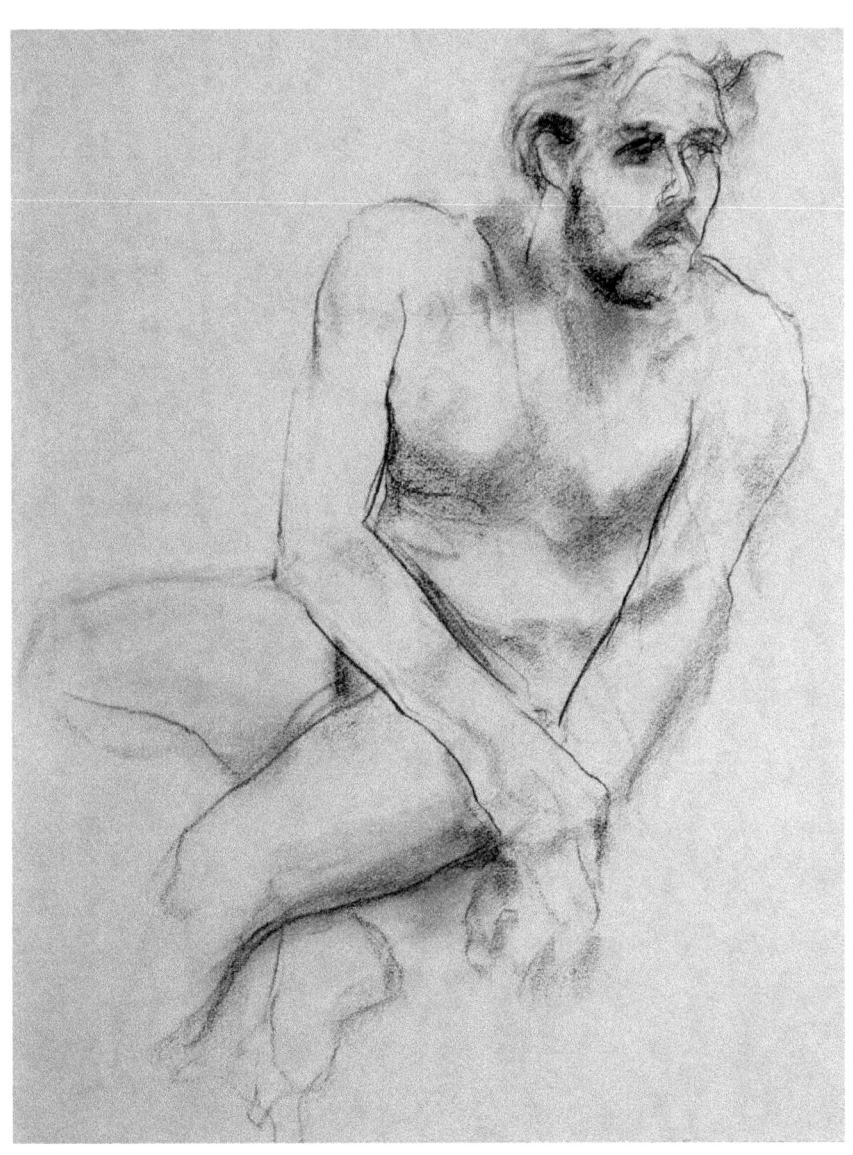

A Place to Pause

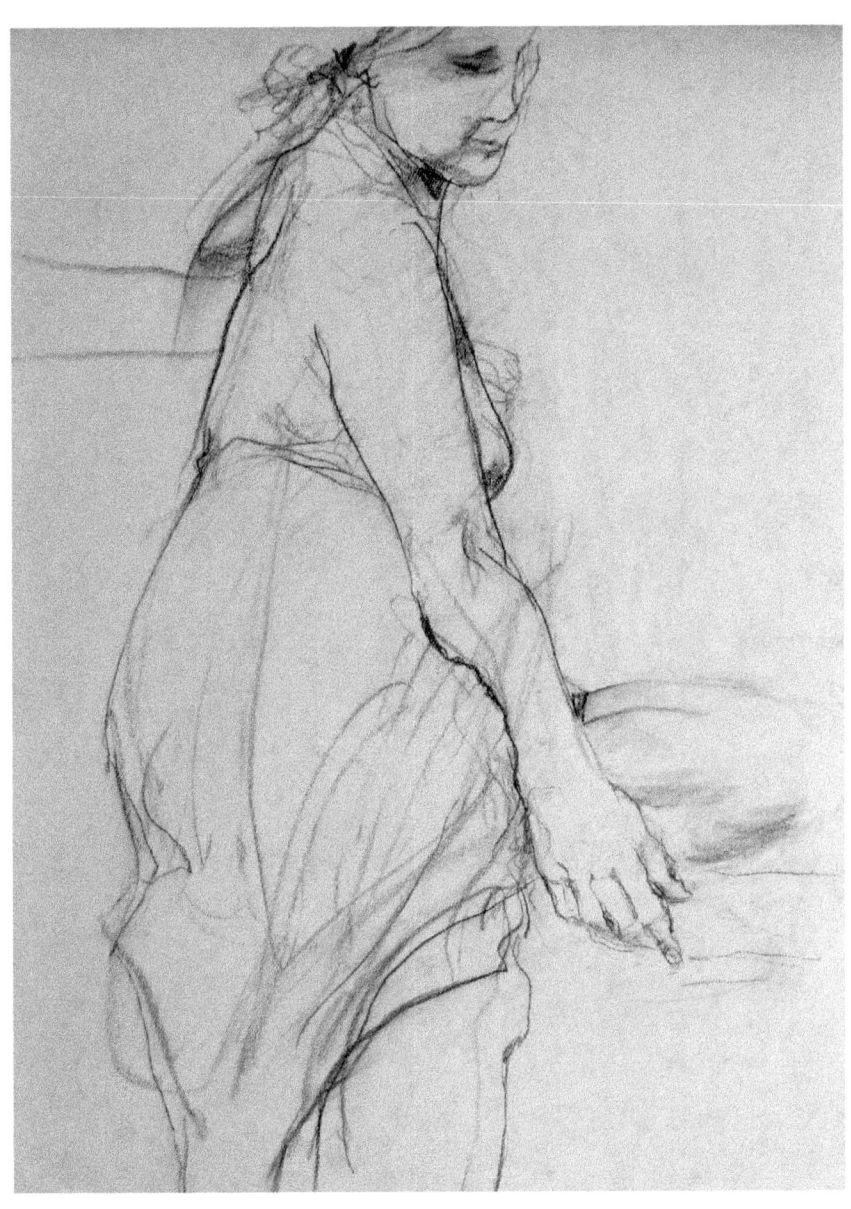

Journey Home

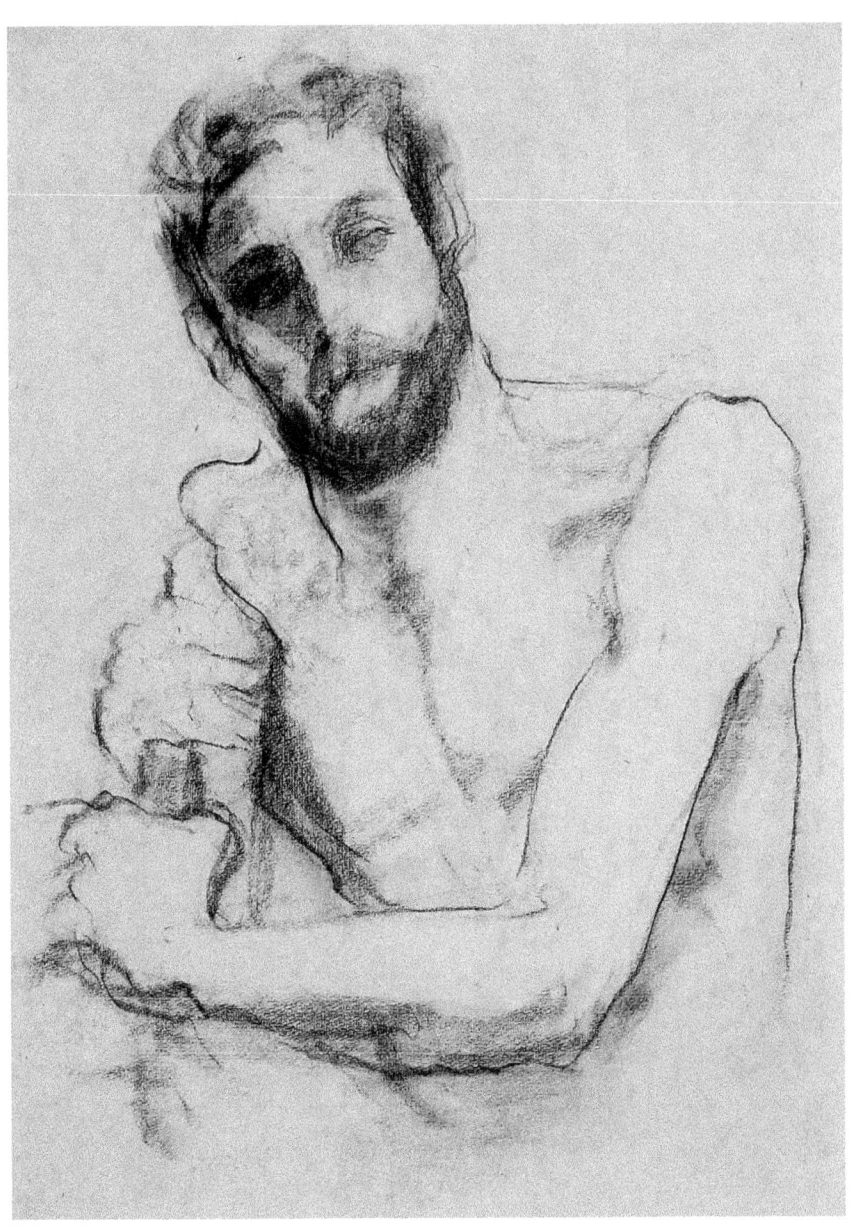

Embracing Life

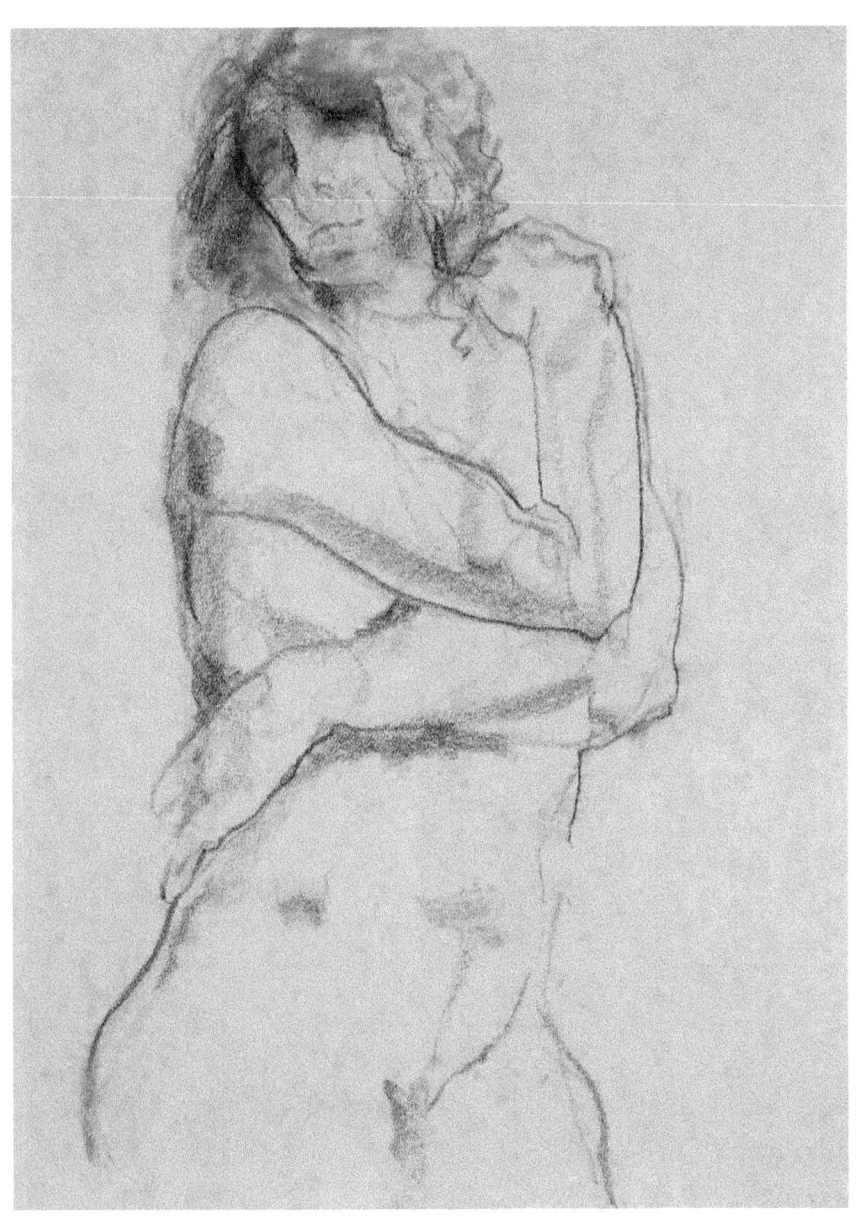

Every Body is Beautiful

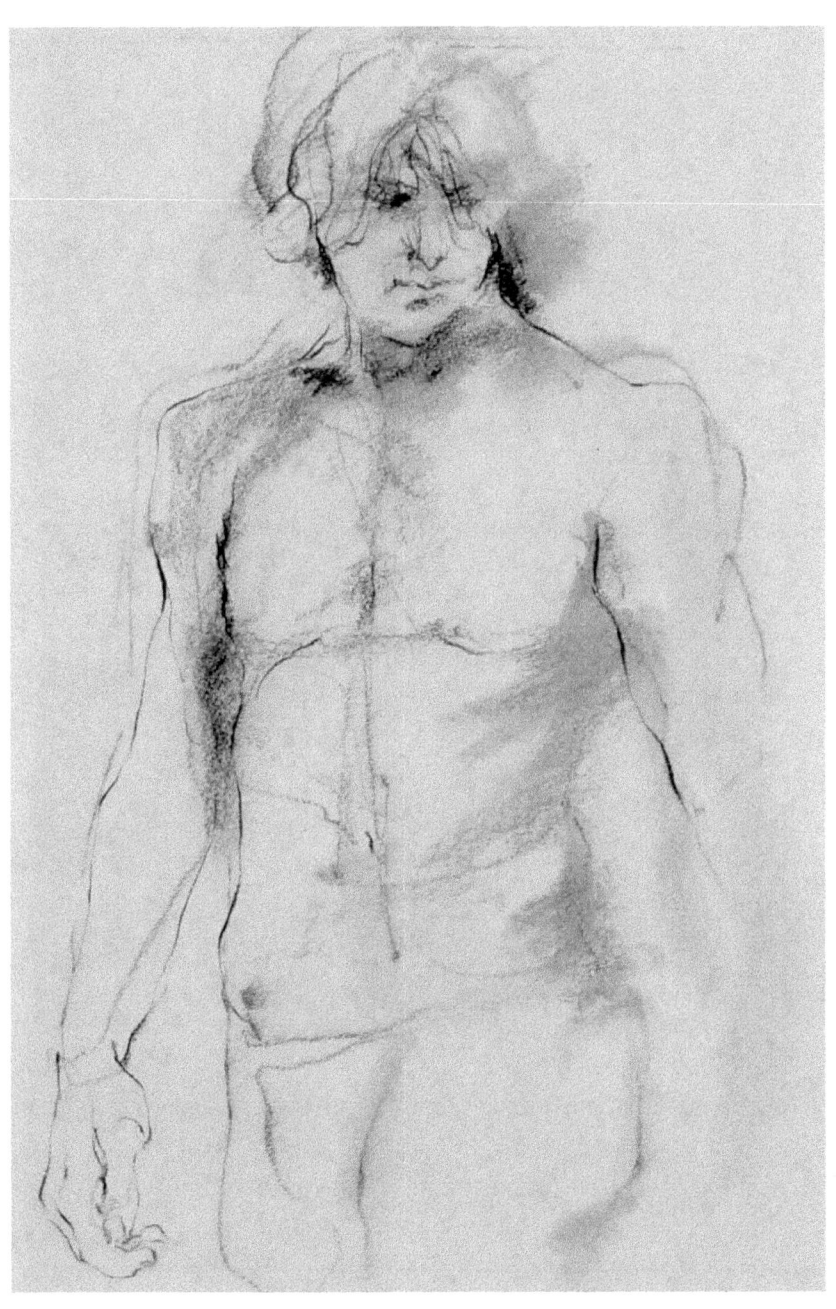

True Nature

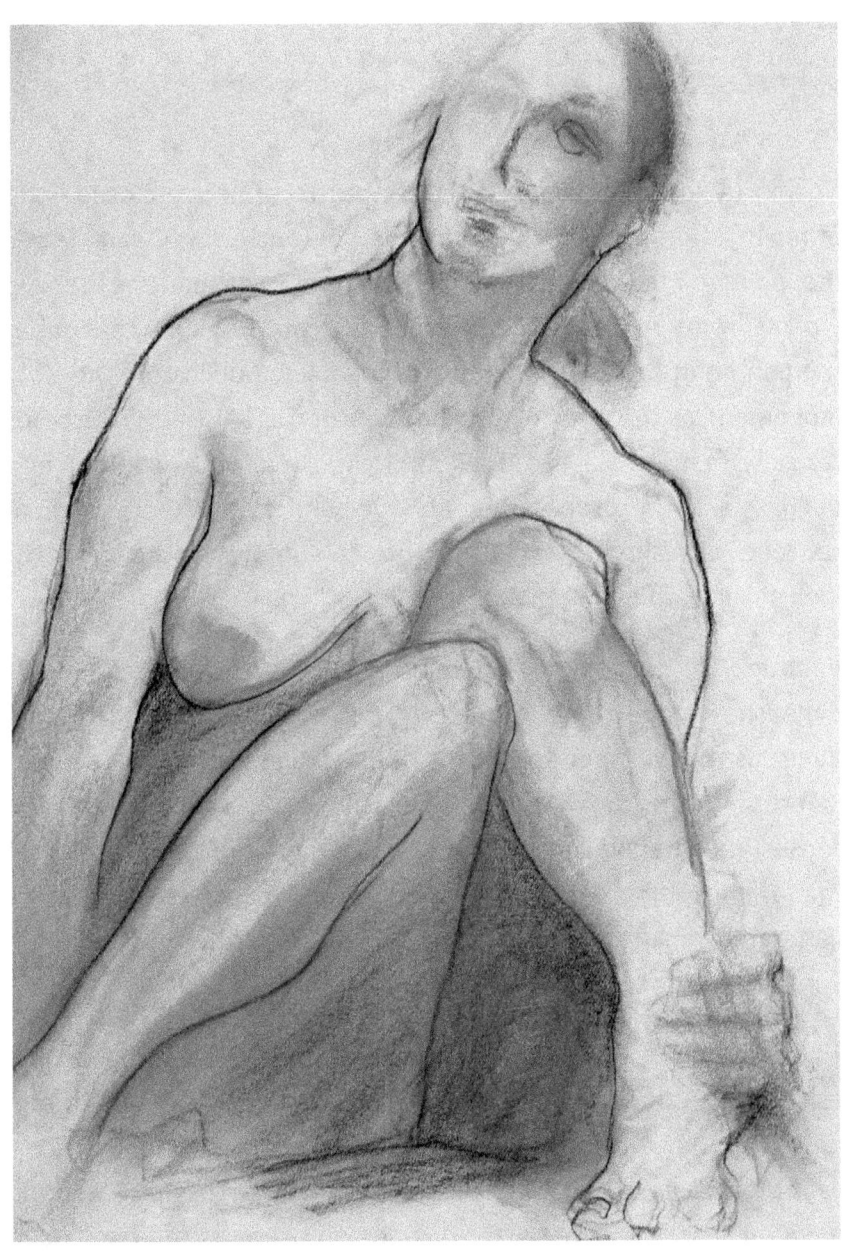

Contour Drawings

I begin by looking at myself in the mirror—one eye closed—the other fixed on a point on an outside contour of my head. That's the point of beginning. Pen in hand, point on paper—the eye looking in the mirror begins to trace the contour. Simultaneously, the pen point on paper begins drawing a line duplicating the slow movement of the eye. When that contour is finished I'm free to take my first look at the drawing. I choose another contour and begin again. The process repeats over and over. When the final contour is finished—I take a minute to summon the courage to look at the result.

Variation in degree of eye movement either exaggerates, or diminishes proportions. If the eye stills the line stops. If the eye quickens the line speeds up. Line quality gives both character and identity to the drawing. The intensity of focus heightens my senses. Heightened senses affect the acuity of the line. The slower the eye movement the more perceptive. Increased perception generates feeling. Escalated feeling tunes into subtle nuances. Subtle nuances refine my sensibility.

The finished drawing is an expression of truth in the moment. It's reality caught in time change. The distortion creates strength and power in the drawing. The finished portrait always a surprise—very often a shock—like it or not—never fails to reveal something of who I am. The most mysterious person I know is the one I have been looking at.

Contour drawing is more than a mindful exercise—it's more than a meditation—it's more than a distorted portrait. *It's a great teacher.*

Contour Drawing

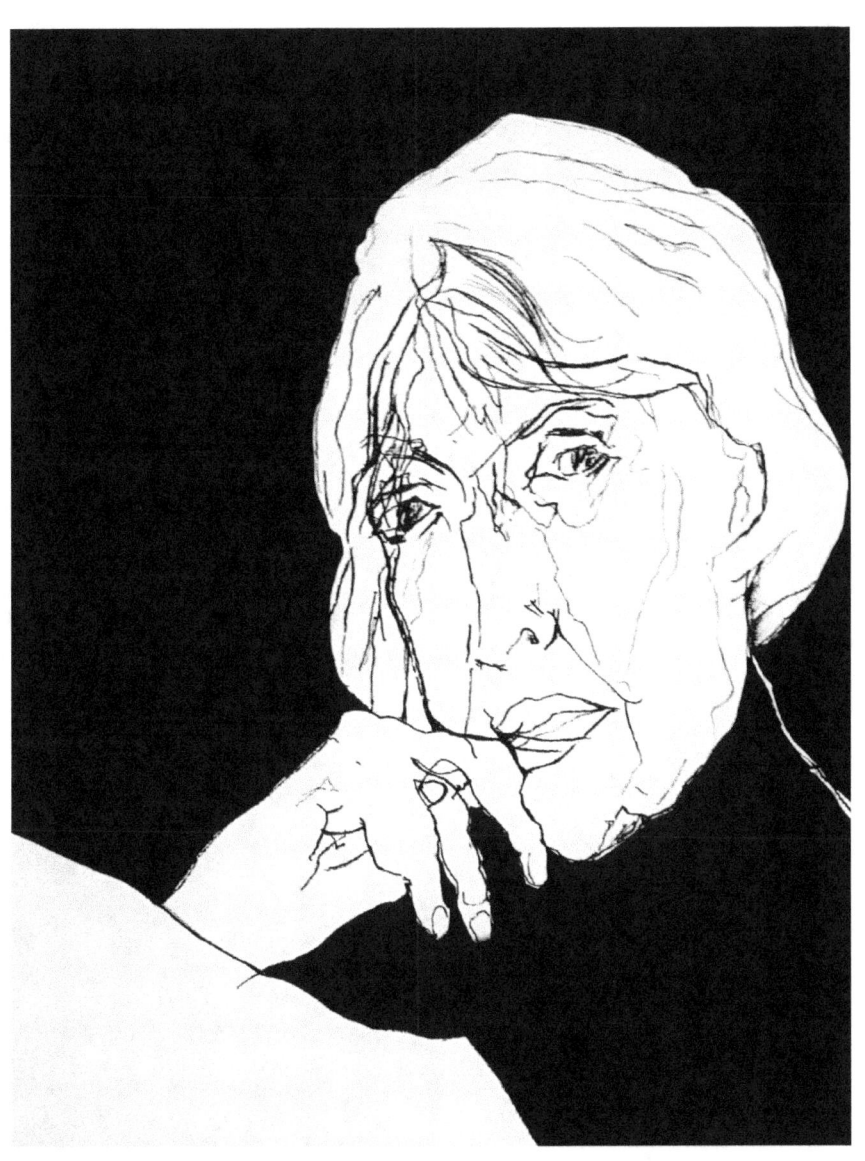

Contour Drawing

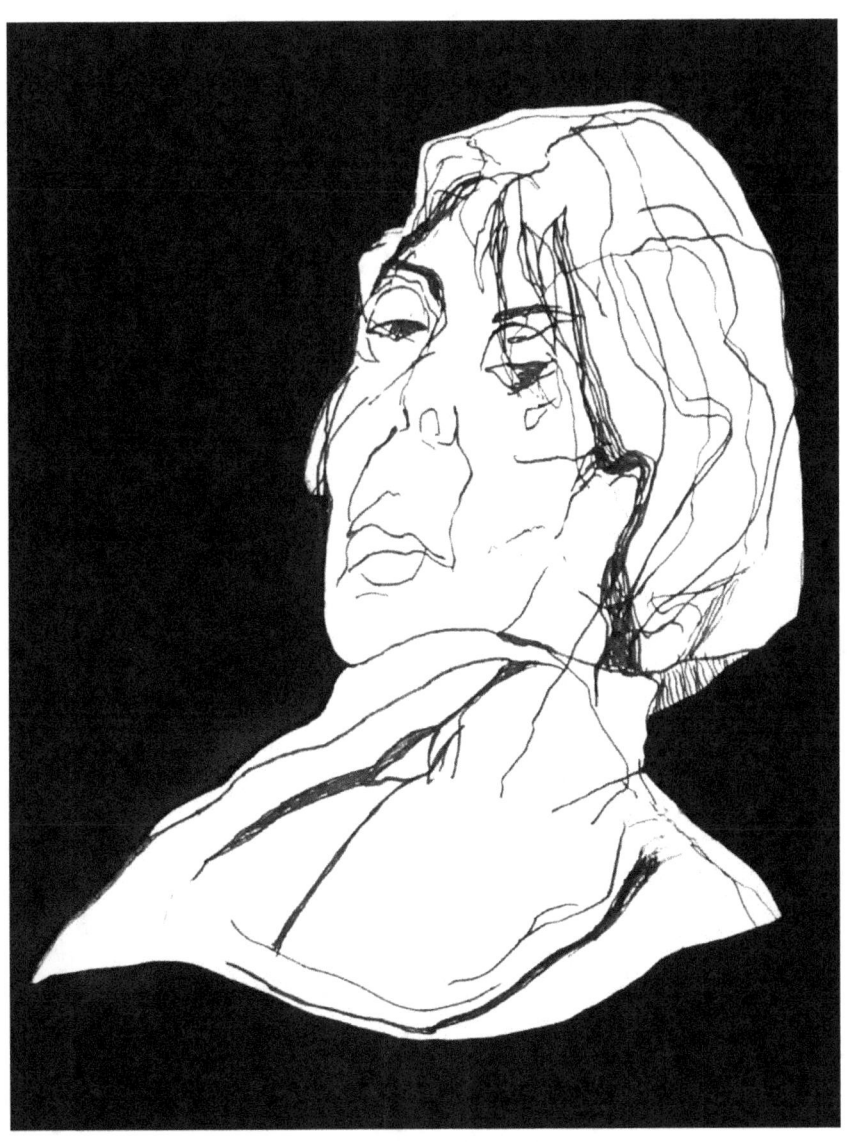

Contour Drawing

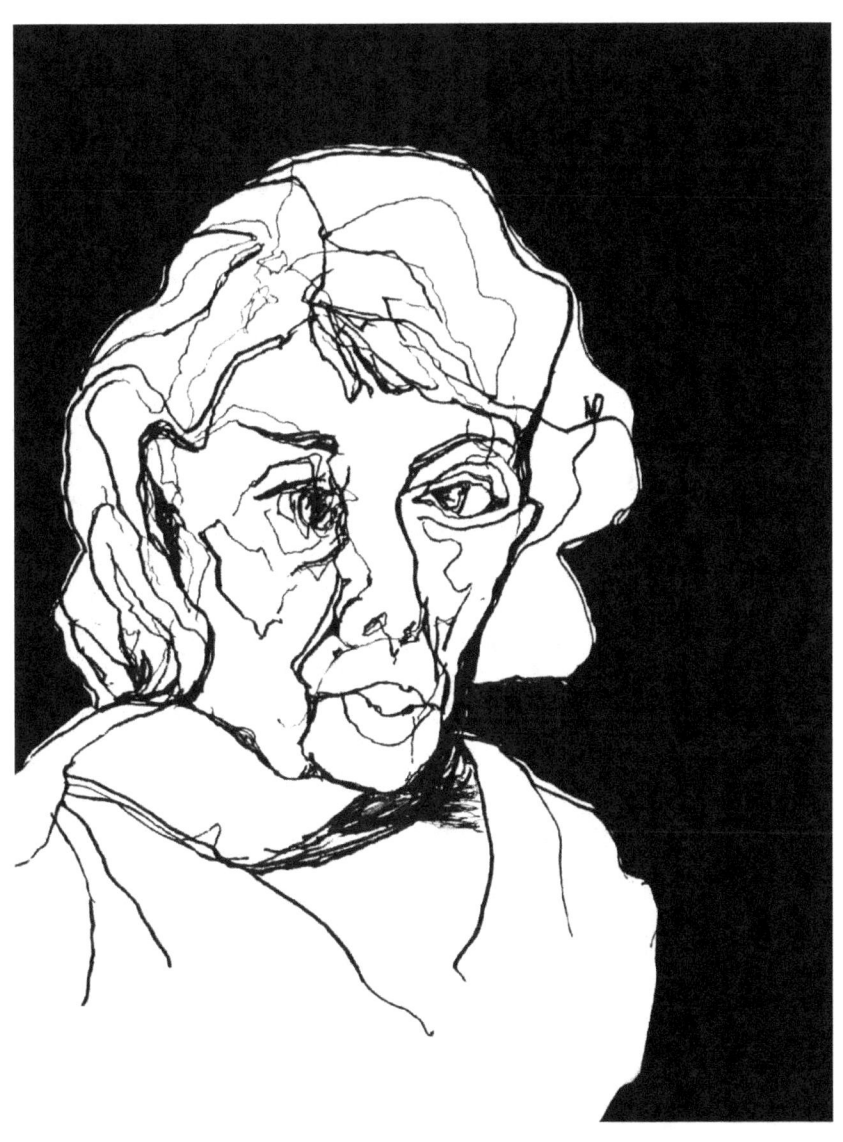

Contour Drawing

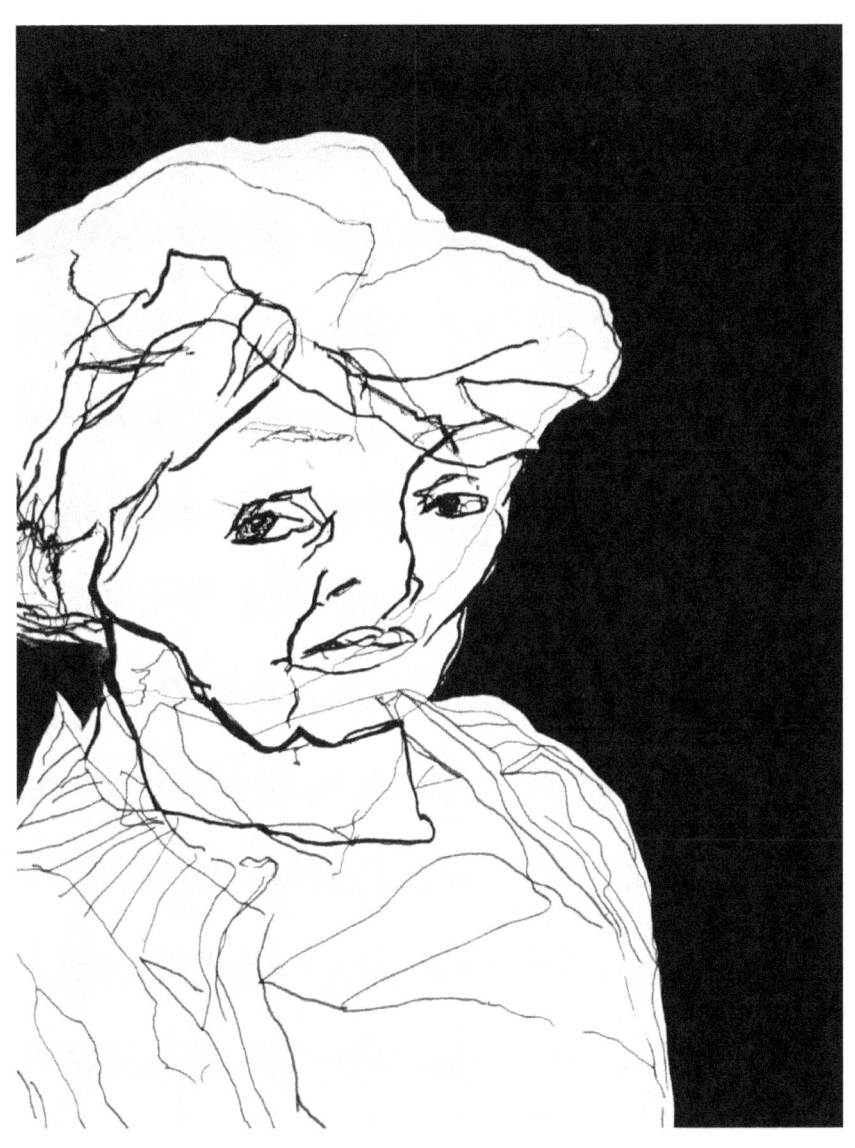

Contour Drawing

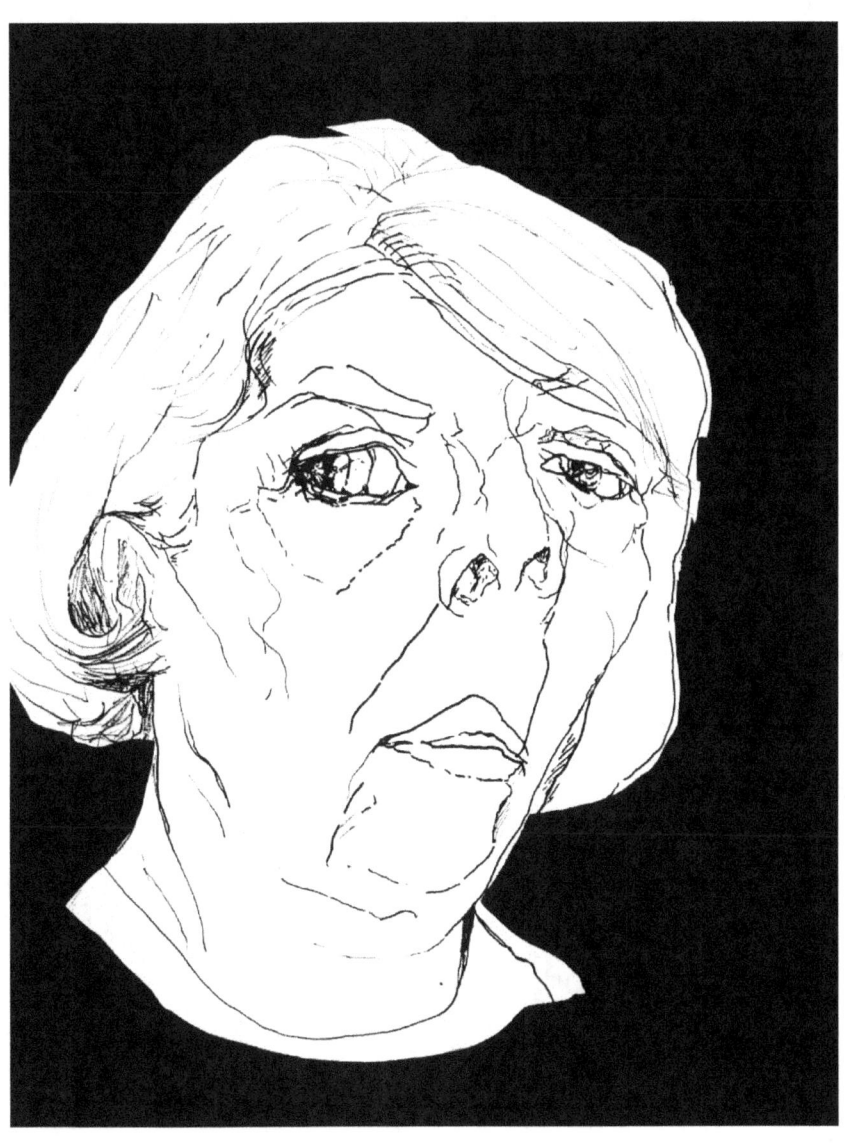

Contour Drawing

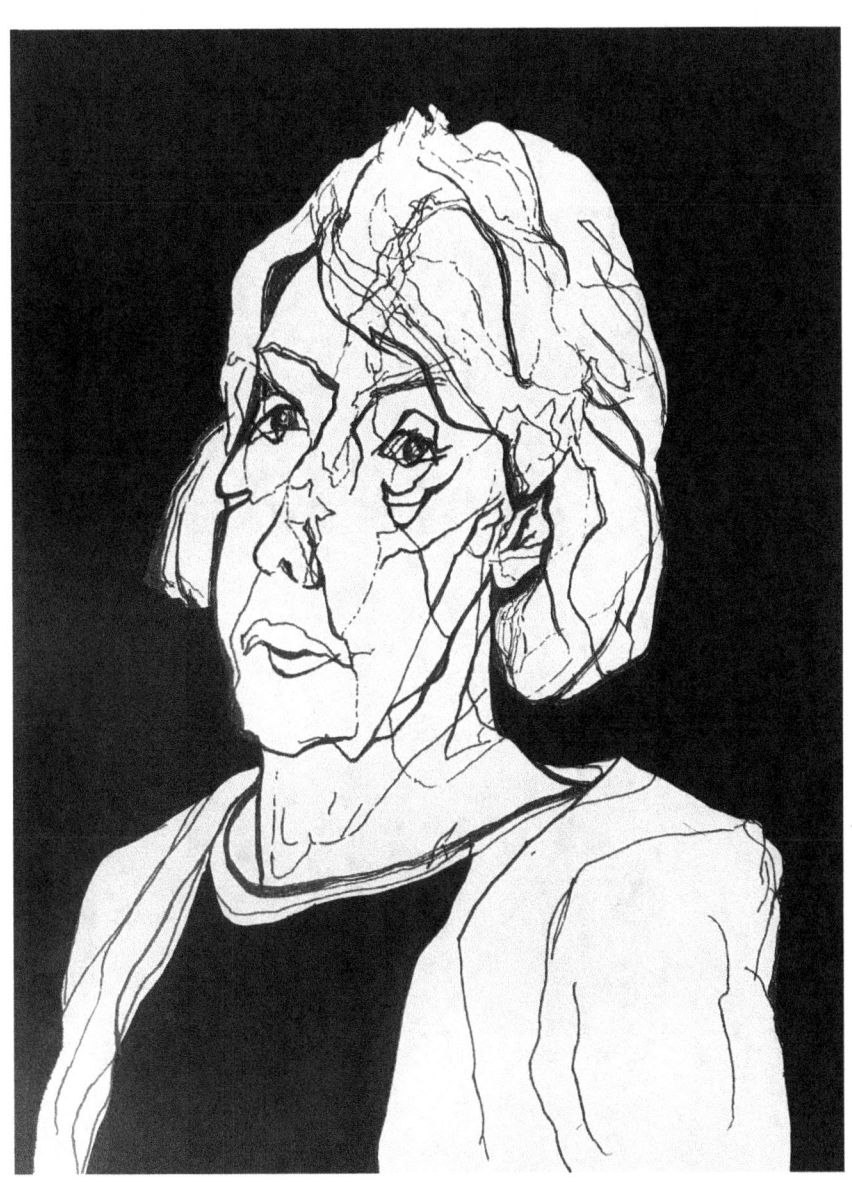

Contour Drawing

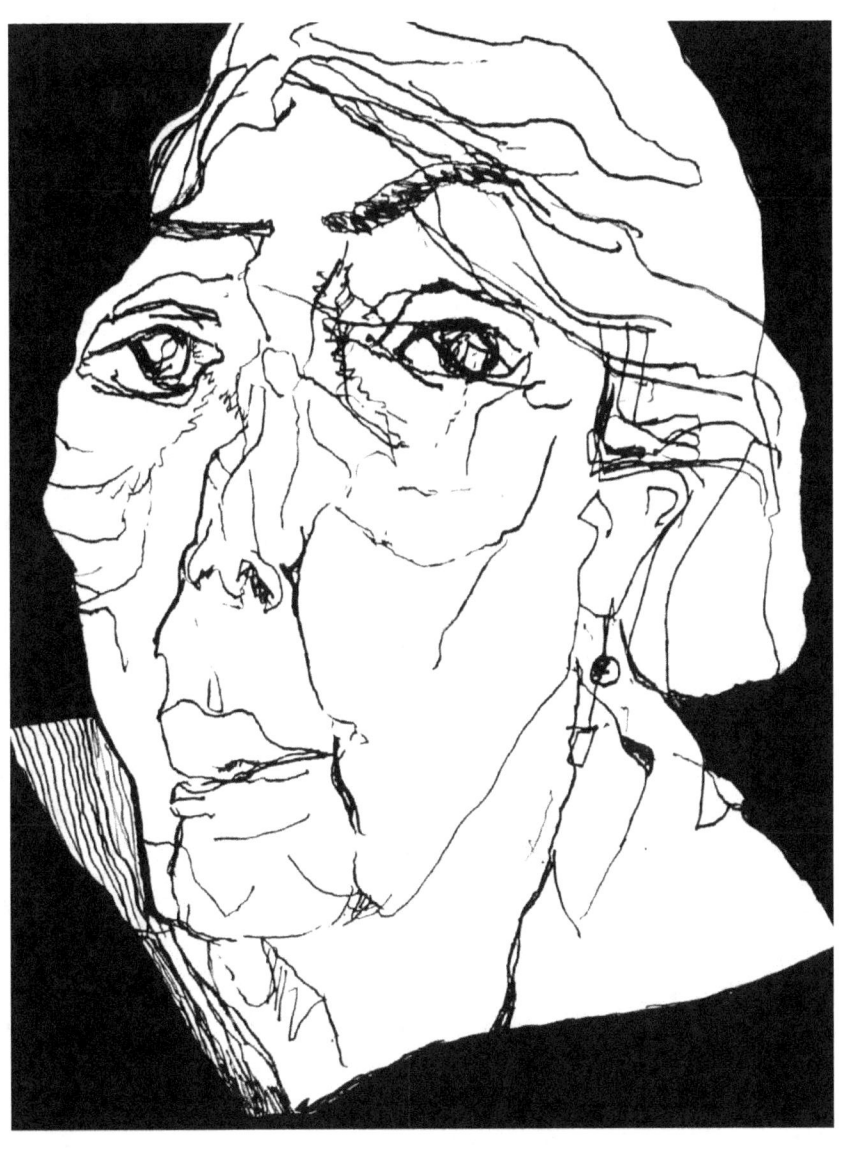

Contour Drawing

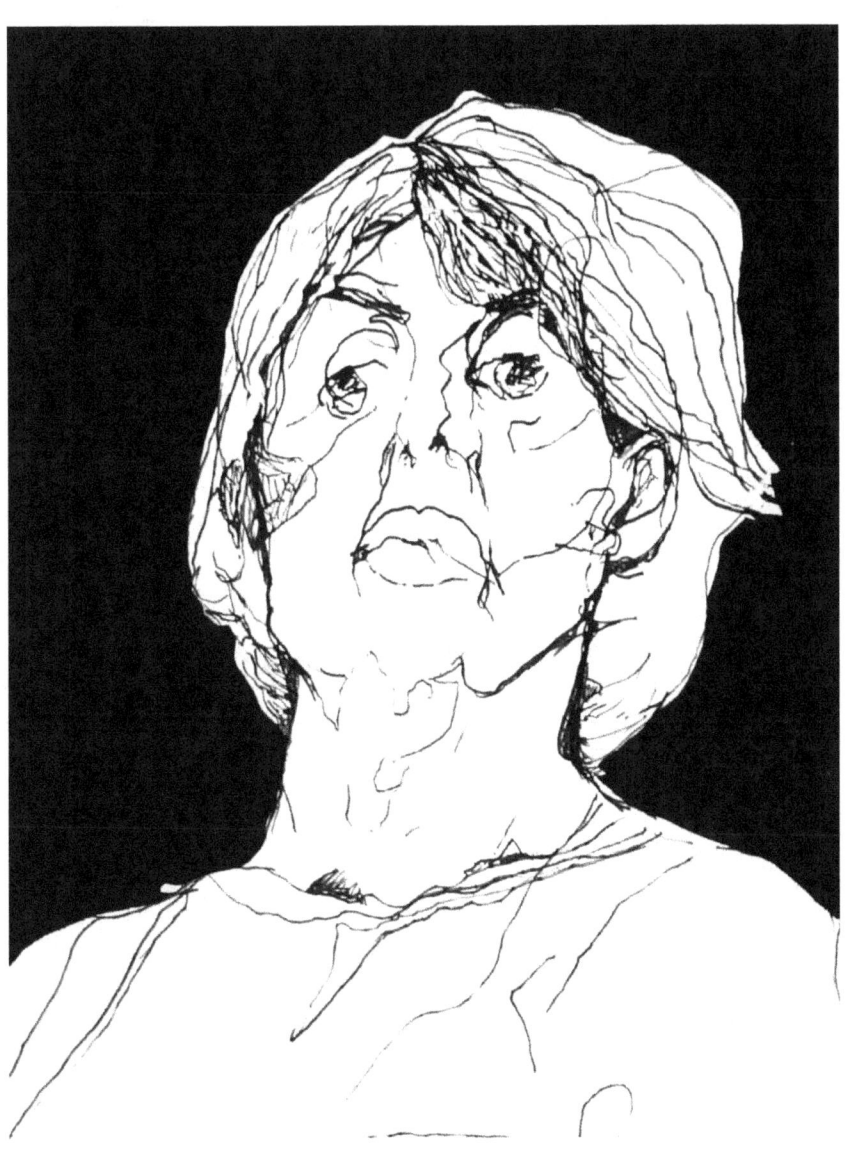

Contour Drawing

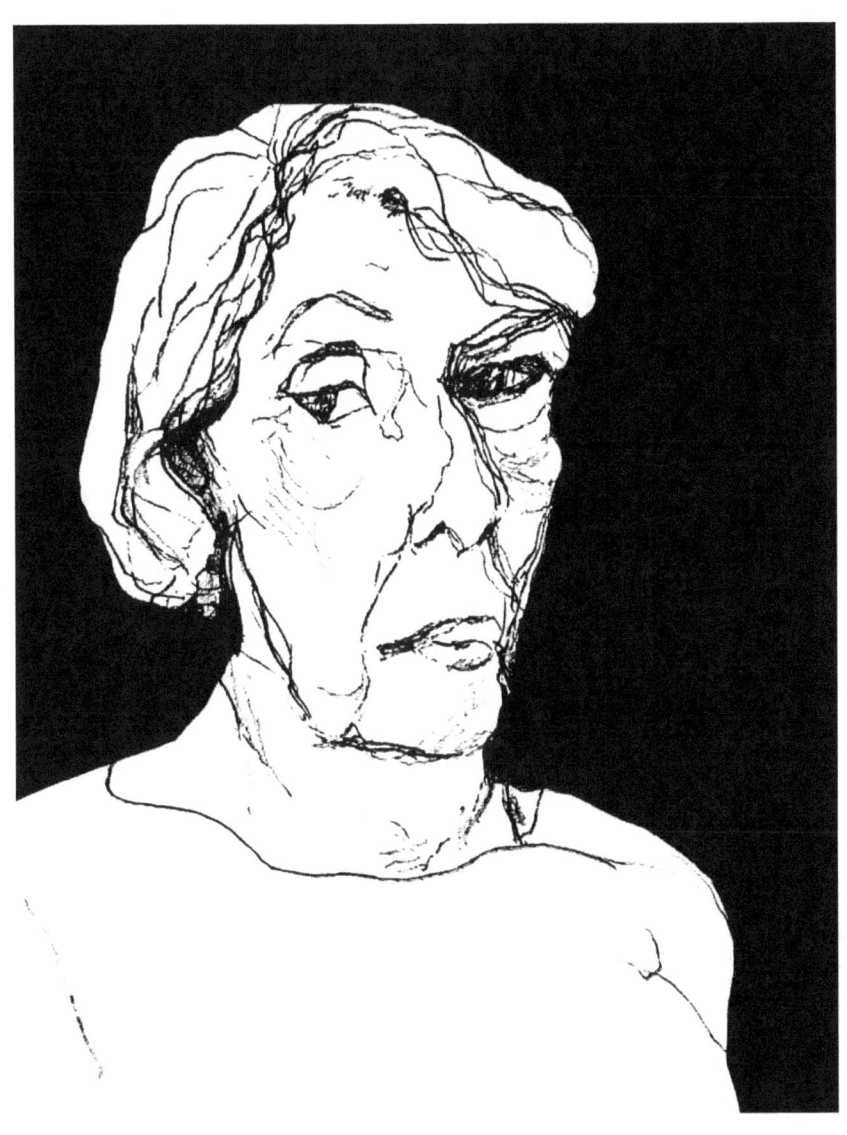

Contour Drawing

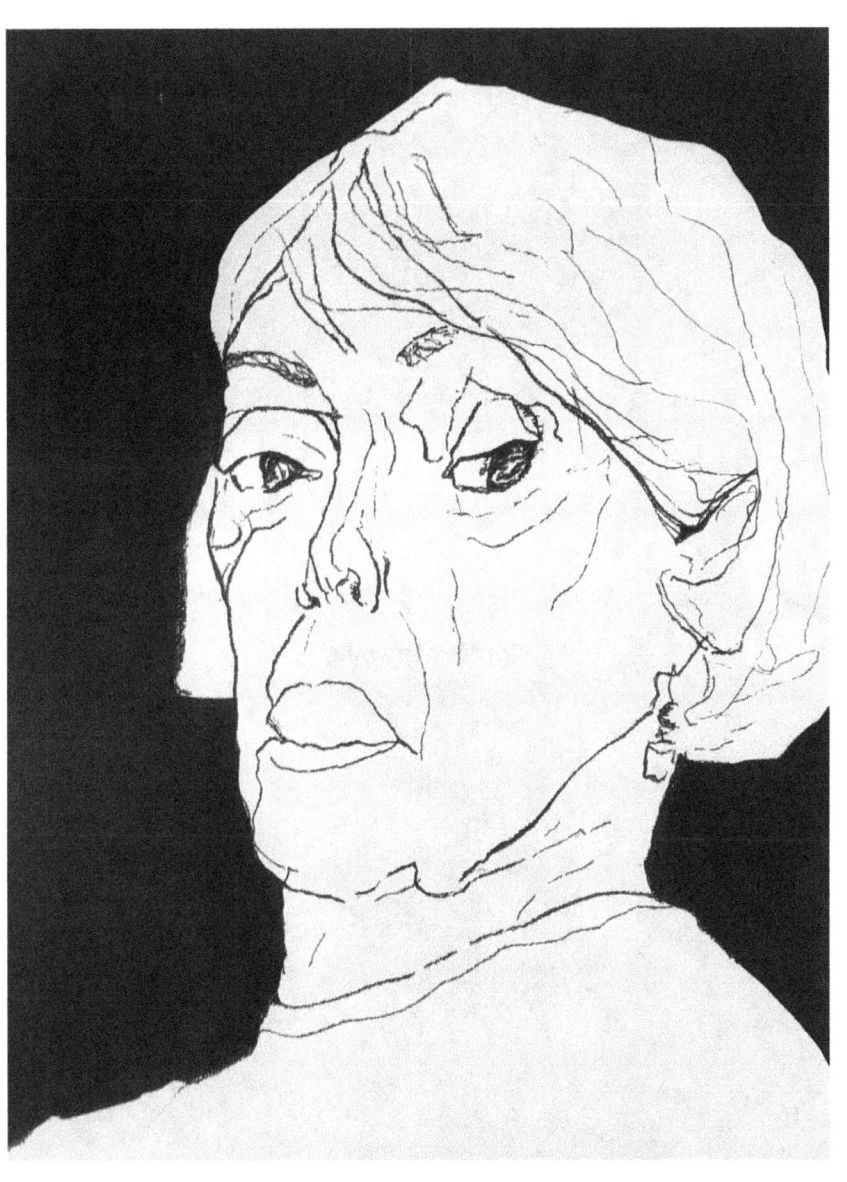

Contour Drawing

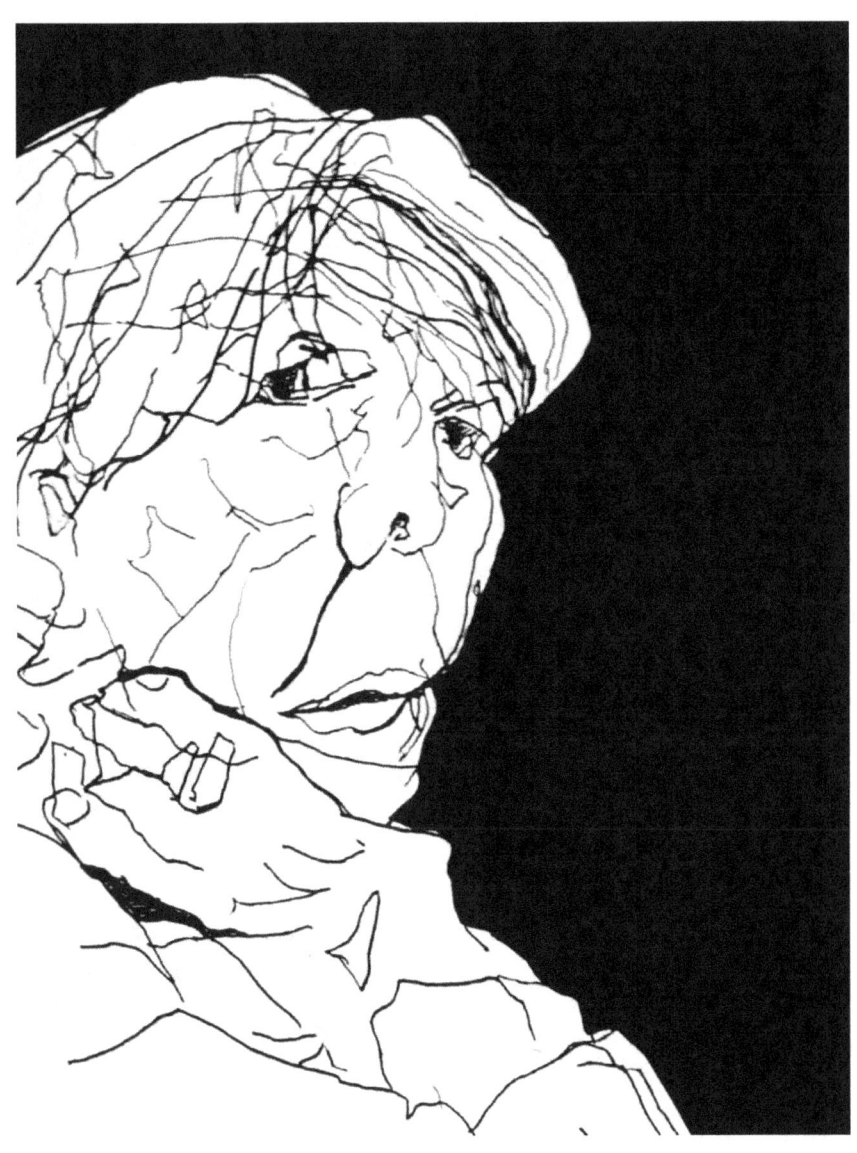

Contour Drawing

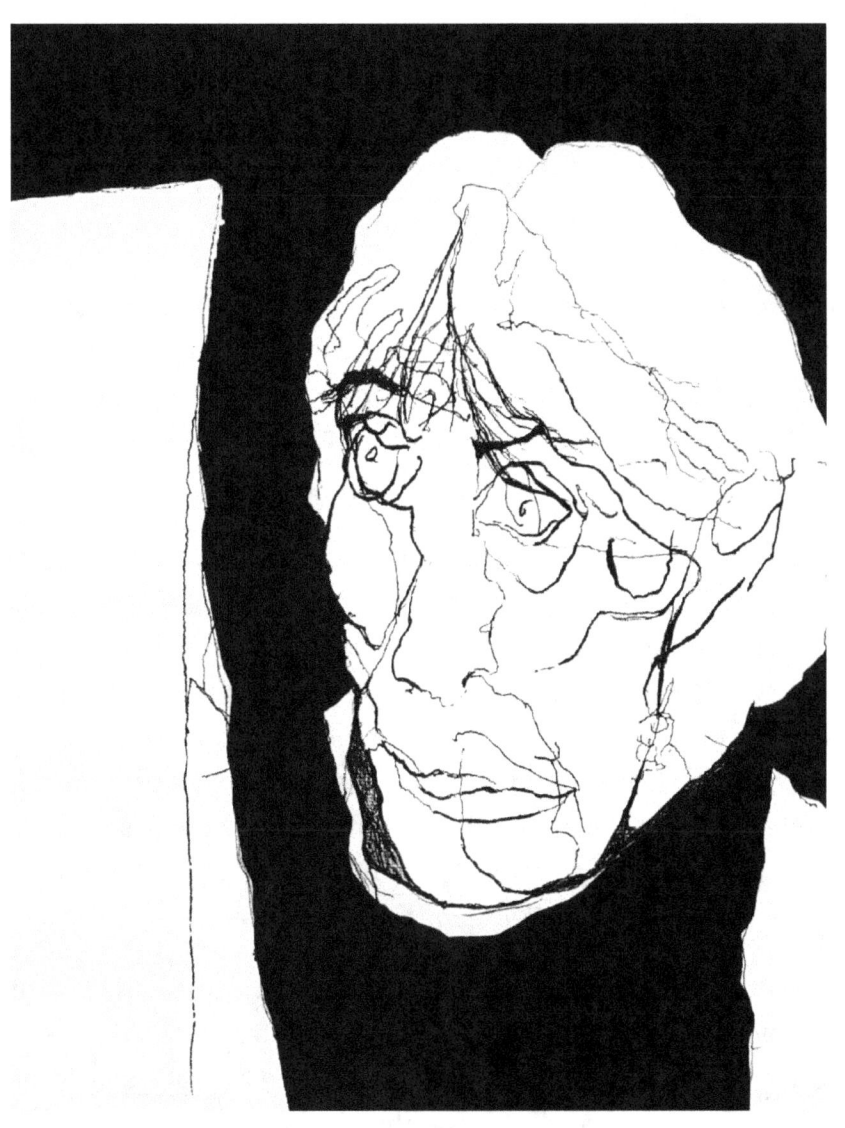

Consciousness and Sub-Consciousness

In a room full of artists, all eyes on the model, all pencils poised, she steps into the spot-light, she takes the pose. Under scrutiny she freezes. Conscious thought carried her into the light. Dark undercurrents cooled her composure. The change, if not seen, is felt.

Consciousness and sub-consciousness are two sides of the same coin—one light, the other dark. Consciousness, objective and rational, works in the light. Sub-consciousness, subjective and emotional, prefers the dark. The model consciously took the pose, sub-consciousness went into hiding. Emotion triggered the fear button. The effect, a divided self, a split between the right and left hemispheres of the brain—the two modes of consciousness. The pose void of feeling freezes. I see the change. I feel the tension. Tense muscles tighten. Tense muscles can't draw.

Respecting the feelings of her soul-mate, she consciously creates an invisible circle—a "safe" zone. She invites her dark side to come into the light. Sub-consciousness, feeling safe and loved, lightens up. Reconciled, she breathes a sigh of relief letting go of the tension. It's clear, consciousness and sub-consciousness—thought and feeling—right and left brain—light and dark—are complementary forces that work together.

I breathe a sigh of relief. I draw.

Copying the Masters

My passion for art has been the magnetic force that has drawn me to museums and galleries in countries throughout the world. At this moment, through the computer, videos, slides, and books, the works of master draftsmen, painters, and sculptors, are at my fingertips. As a result, I have been able to see great art and apprentice with the greatest artists of all time.

When I was nine years old, I fell in love with the figure drawings of Michelangelo. I was making a scrapbook about the story of "Paul on the Road to Damascus." One of Michelangelo's figures became the image I used for Paul. I came upon the image in one of the encyclopedias my parents had ordered from a door to door salesman. Stepping out of those pages and into my life Michelangelo became my first art teacher. Over the years, I have copied many of his drawings and paintings. It was no surprise to me that I felt so at home in Rome gazing at the ceiling of the Sistine Chapel. I knew all those images. They were almost like family to me. Michelangelo remains a major teacher in my life today.

Choosing a work of art I'm drawn to I do my utmost to imitate it. After having had the experience and have allowed time for the information to gel, I let it go. Later, I'm aware that something happened. The old and the new fused. My sensibilities are more informed. My perception is sharpened. My ability is enhanced. Copying provides the synthesis that expands my awareness.

For the geometry classes in high school, I made copies of

figurative paintings from the works of Renaissance artists. Another student diagrammed the underlying geometric structure of each composition. Some of the master artists that I copied were da Vinci, Raphael, Rubens, Titian, Botticelli, as well as Michelangelo. The works of those artists were major influences that further enhanced my aesthetic sensibility. In recent years, I have copied drawings of Gauguin, Van Gogh, Cézanne, Degas, Schiele, and more. The sensitivity and power of their unique lines, forms, colors, textures, and compositions are alive and engraved in my being. I am forever grateful to all of them—my teachers to this day.

Getting stuck in my own comfort zone—in what is acceptable and safe—is stifling. It's necessary to take risks—to keep pushing the envelope. Repeating myself is about fear. Fear is about insecurity. Insecurity is inherent in creativity. Creativity is about change. I want to spread my wings, be spontaneous, trust in the process, and maybe I'll reach the next plateau.

AFTER THE MASTERS

Joyce Eakins
After Leonardo da Vinci (1452-1519)
Old Man
Burndy Library, Norwalk, Connecticut

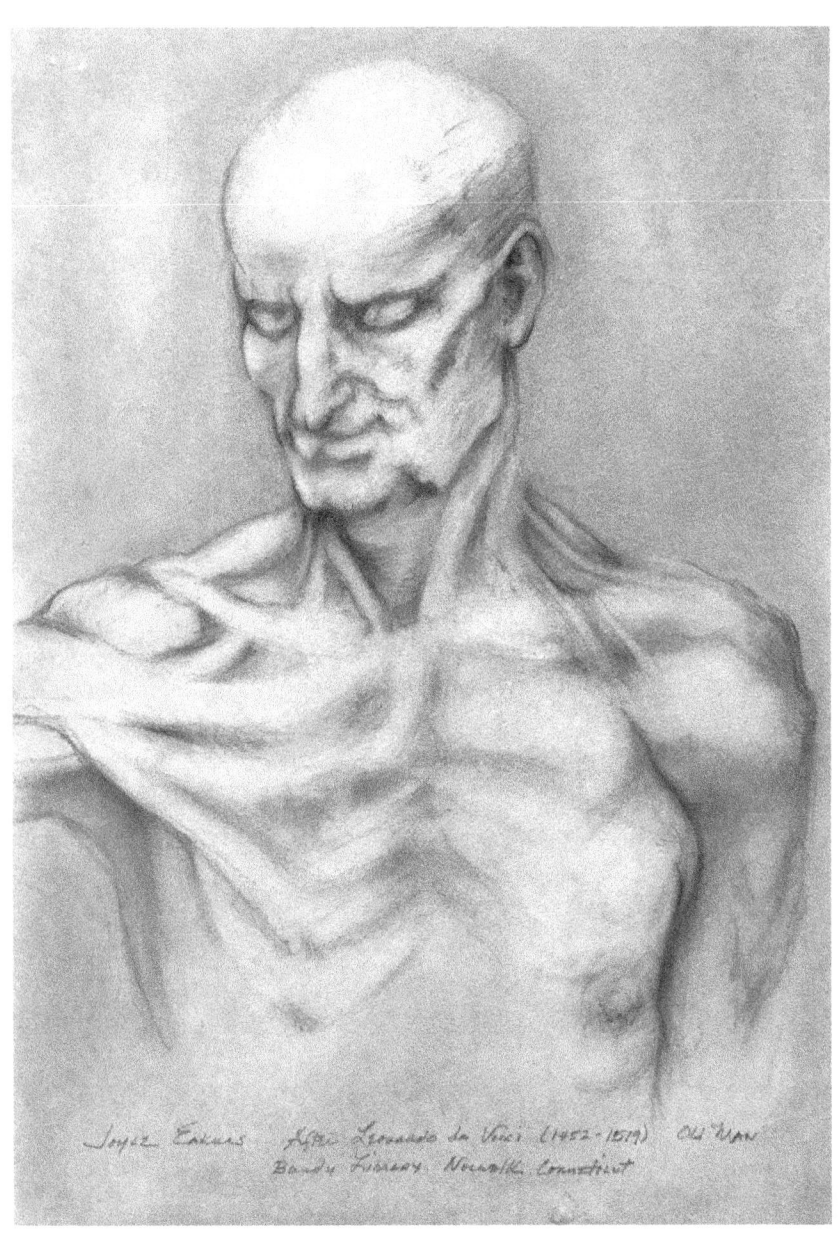

Joyce Eakins   After Leonardo da Vinci (1452-1519)   Old Man
Bowery Library, Norwalk, Connecticut

Joyce Eakins
After Leonardo da Vinci (1452-1519)
Old Man
Burndy Library, Norwalk, Connecticut

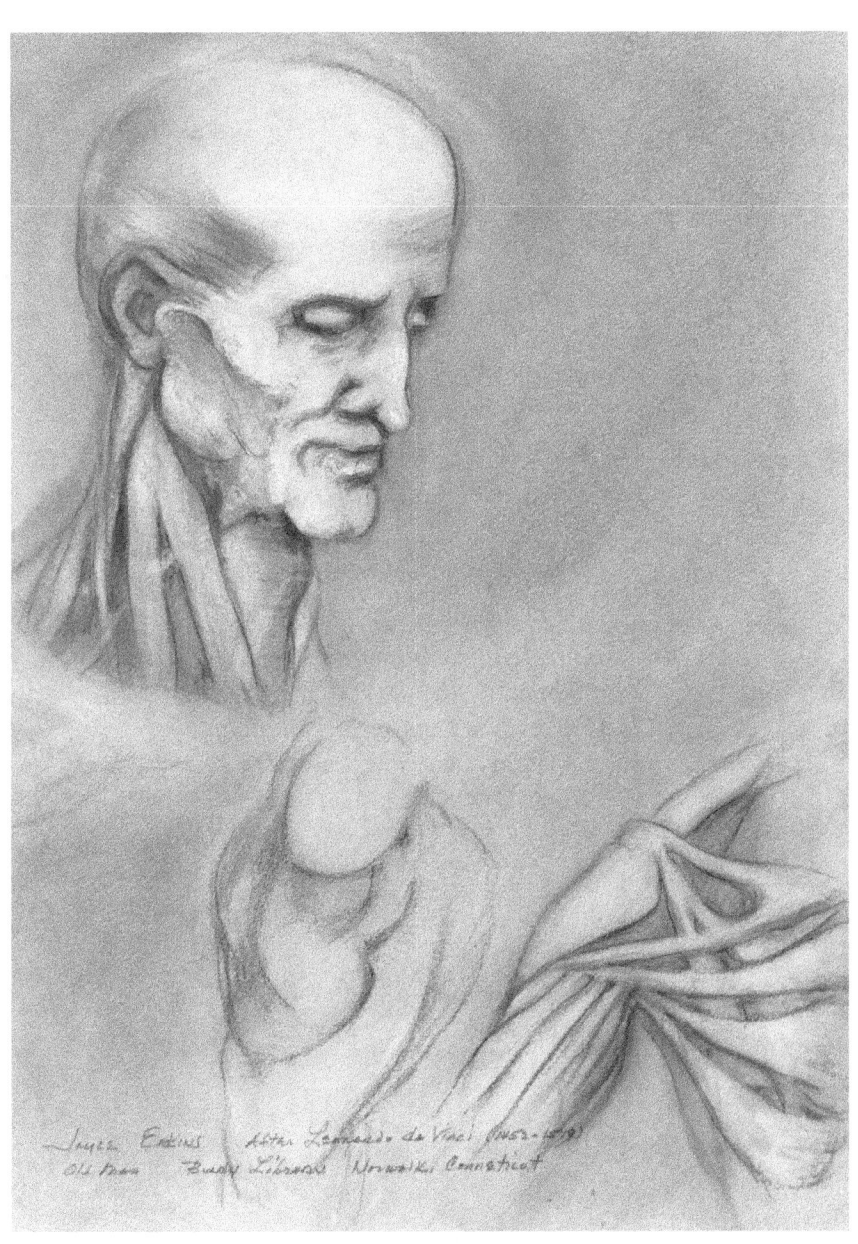

Joyce Erkins   After Leonardo da Vinci (1452-1519)
Old Man   Bush Library Norwalk Connecticut

145

Joyce Eakins
After Leonardo da Vinci (1452-1519)
Old Man, muscles and surface anatomy
Burndy Library, Norwalk, Connecticut

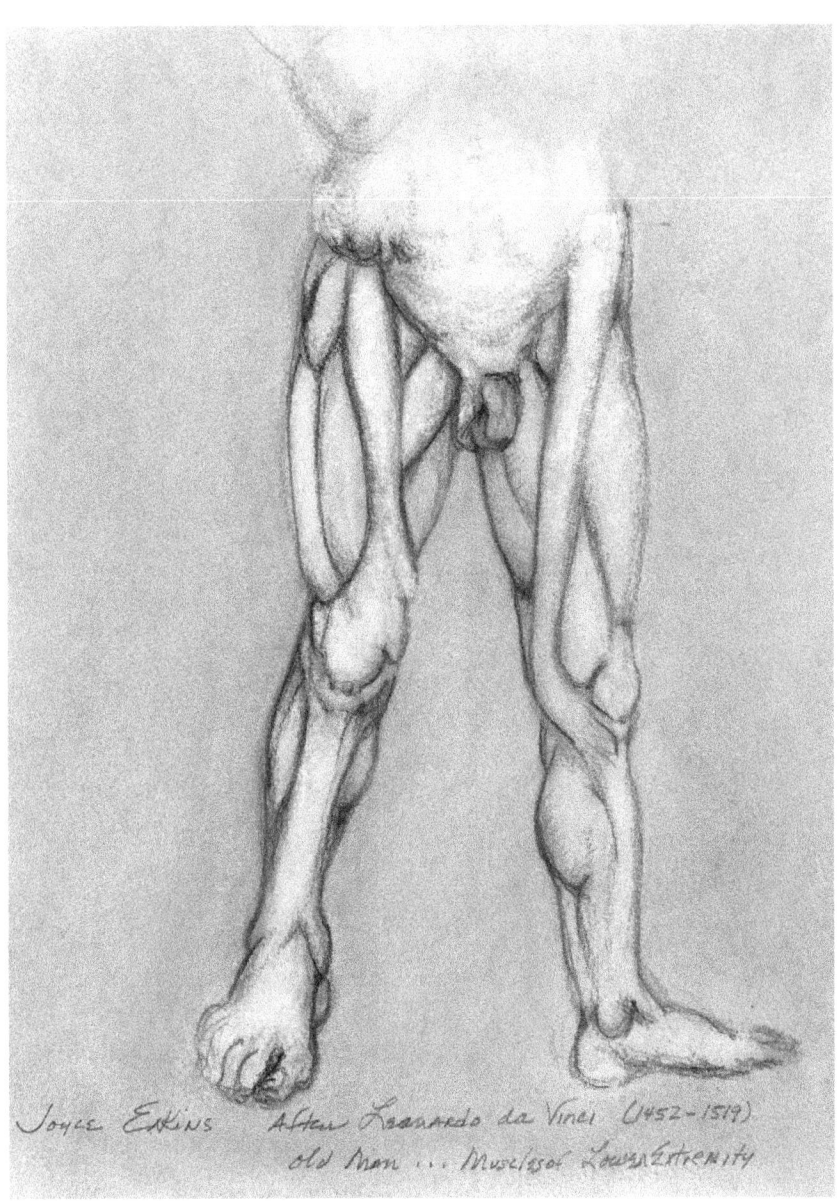

Joyce Elkins   After Leonardo da Vinci (1452-1519)
old Man ... Muscles of Lower Extremity

Joyce Eakins
After Leonardo da Vinci (1452-1519)
Old Man, muscles and surface anatomy
Burndy Library, Norwalk, Connecticut

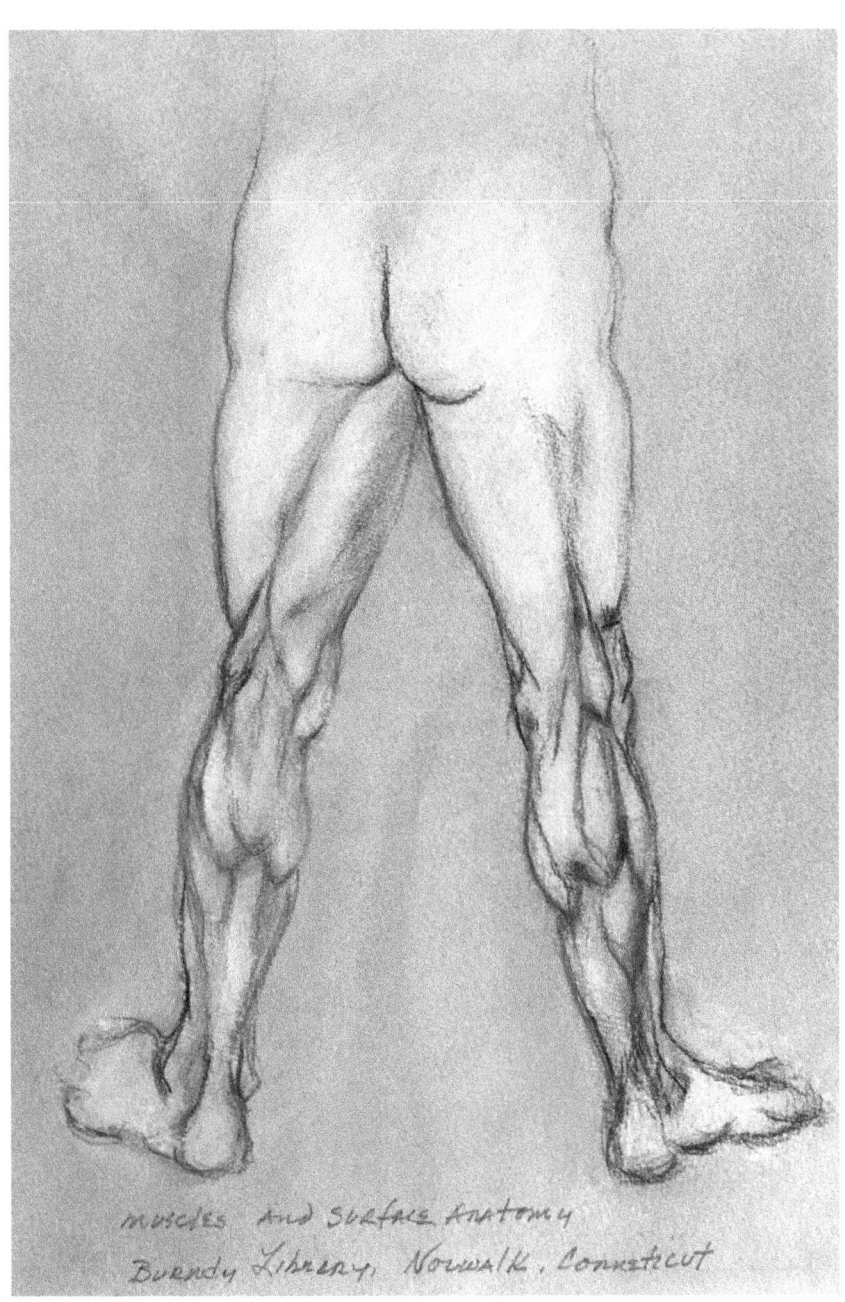

muscles and surface anatomy
Burndy Library, Norwalk, Connecticut

Joyce Eakins
After Michelangelo Buonarroti (1475-1564)
Reclining Male Nude
British Museum, London

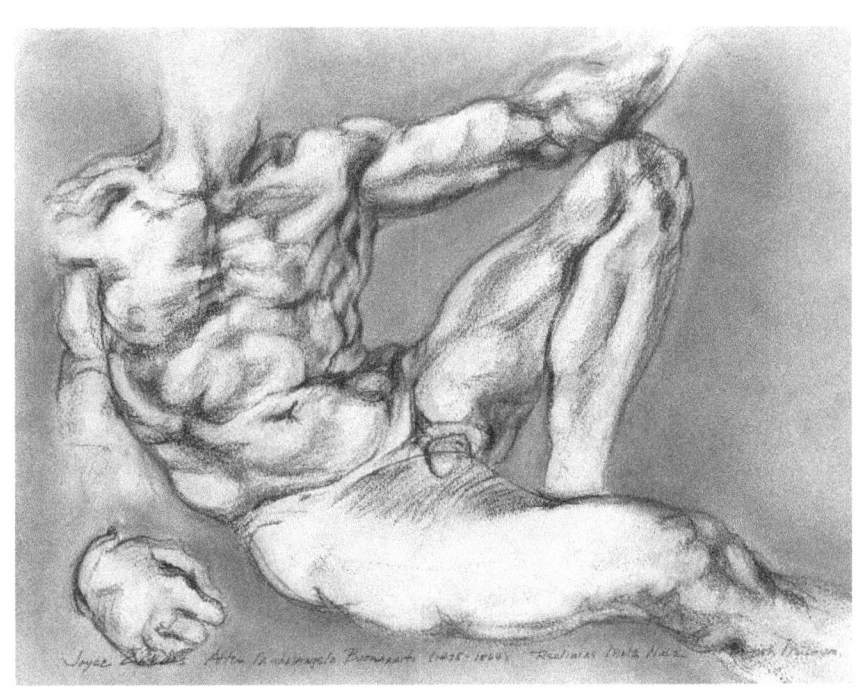

Joyce .... After Michelangelo Buonarroti (1475-1564) "Reclining Nude" ....

Joyce Eakins
After Michelangelo Buonarroti (1474-1564)
Study for Libyan Sibyl
Metropolitan Museum, New York

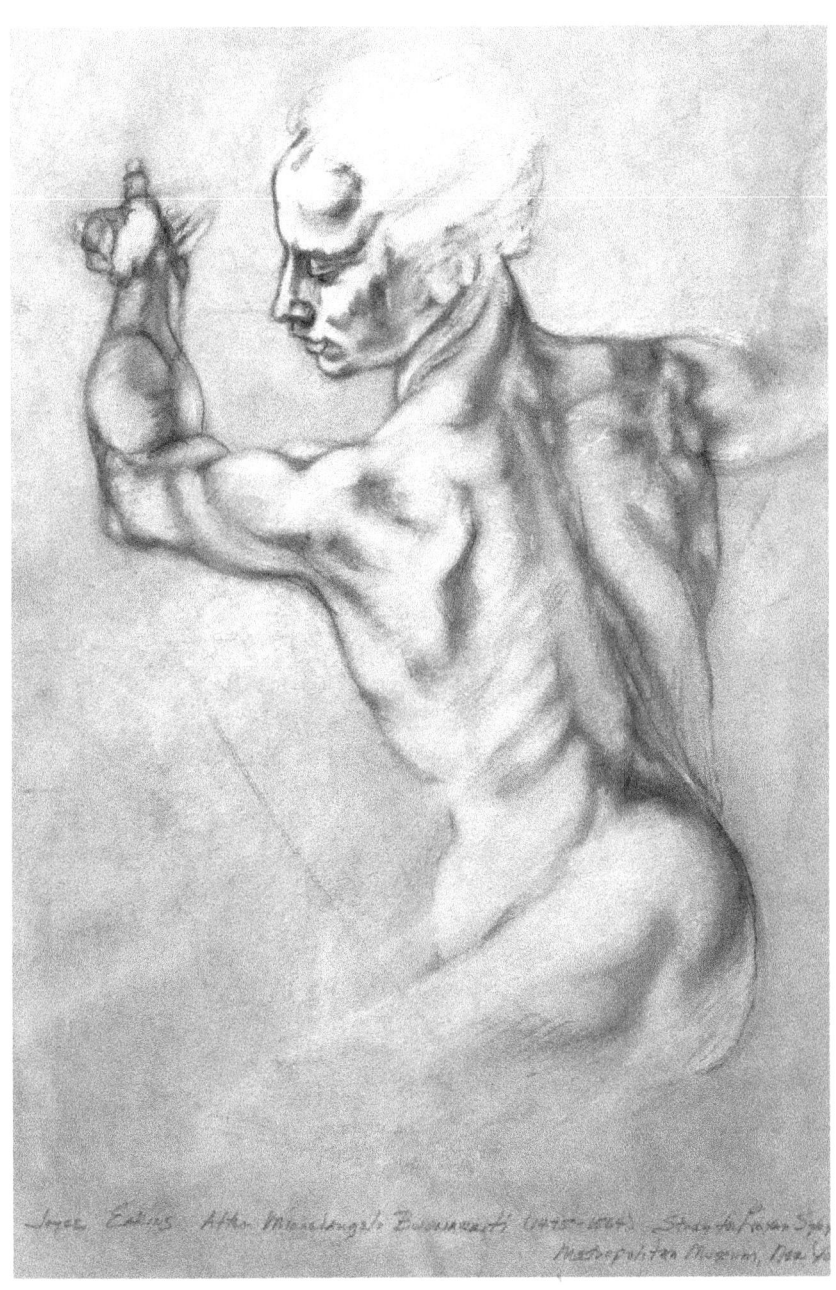

Joyce Eakins   After Michelangelo Buonarroti (1475-1564)   Study for Haman Study
Metropolitan Museum, New York

Joyce Eakins
After Raphael Sanzio (1483-1520)
Female Nude
Tyler Museum, Haarlem, The Netherlands

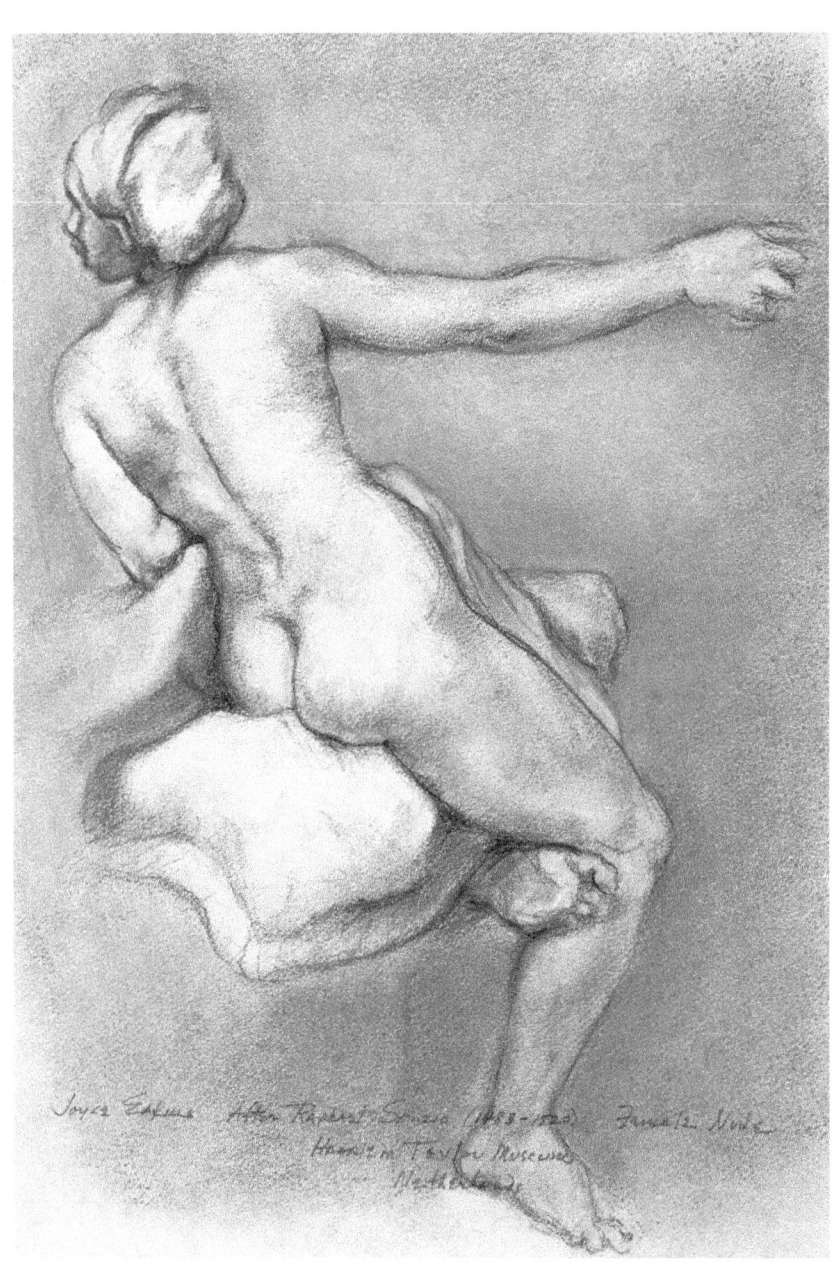

Joyce Erkine   Helen Pinkert-Soricea (1858-1920)   Female Nude
Haarlem Fan for Museum
Netherlands

Joyce Eakins
After Raphael Sanzio (1483-1520)
Men in Combat (Detail)
Ashmolean Museum, Oxford

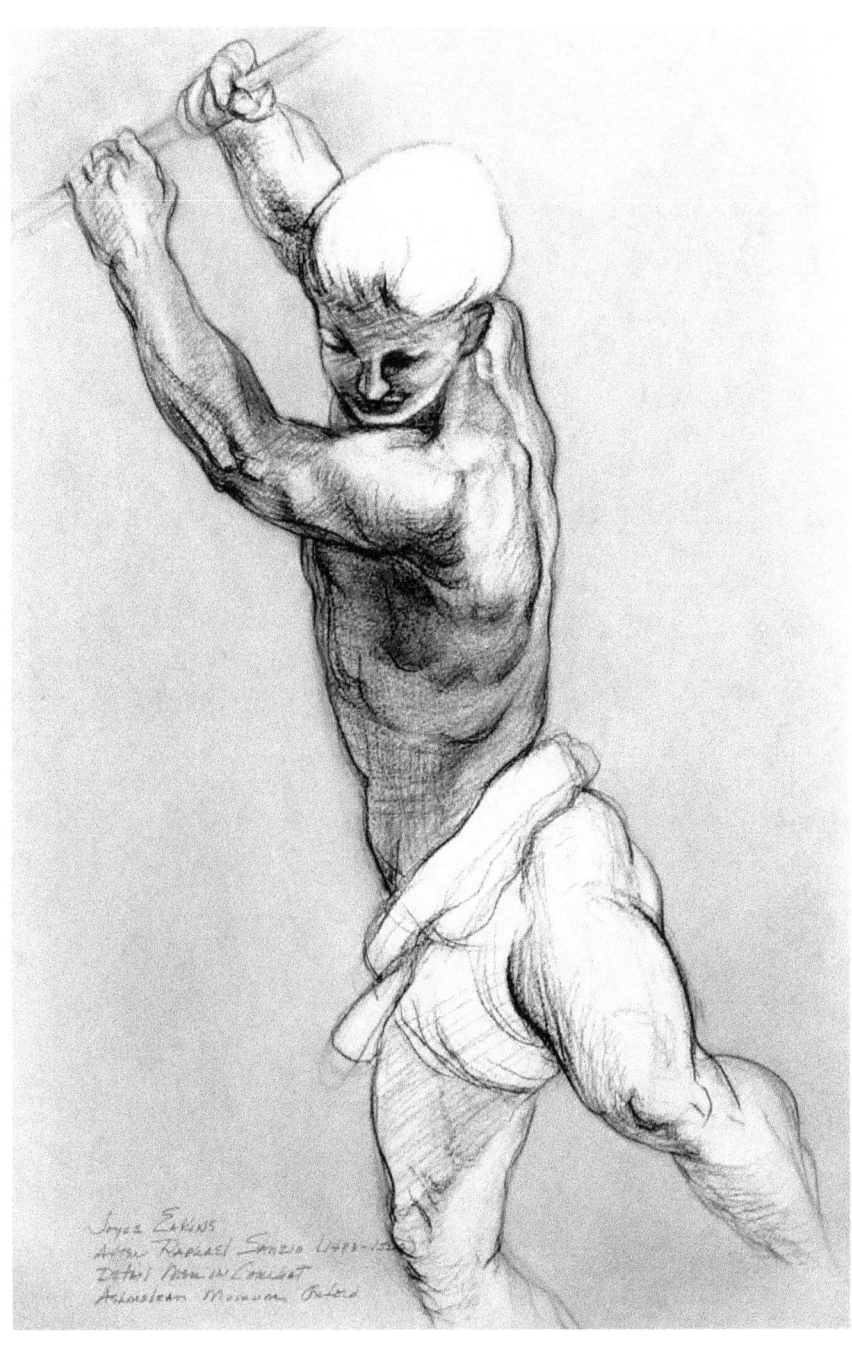

Joyce Eakins
After Raphael Sanzio Urbino
Detail from a Combat
Ashmolean Museum Oxford

157

Joyce Eakins
After Sandro Botticelli
The Birth of Venus (1480)
Uffizi Gallery, Florence

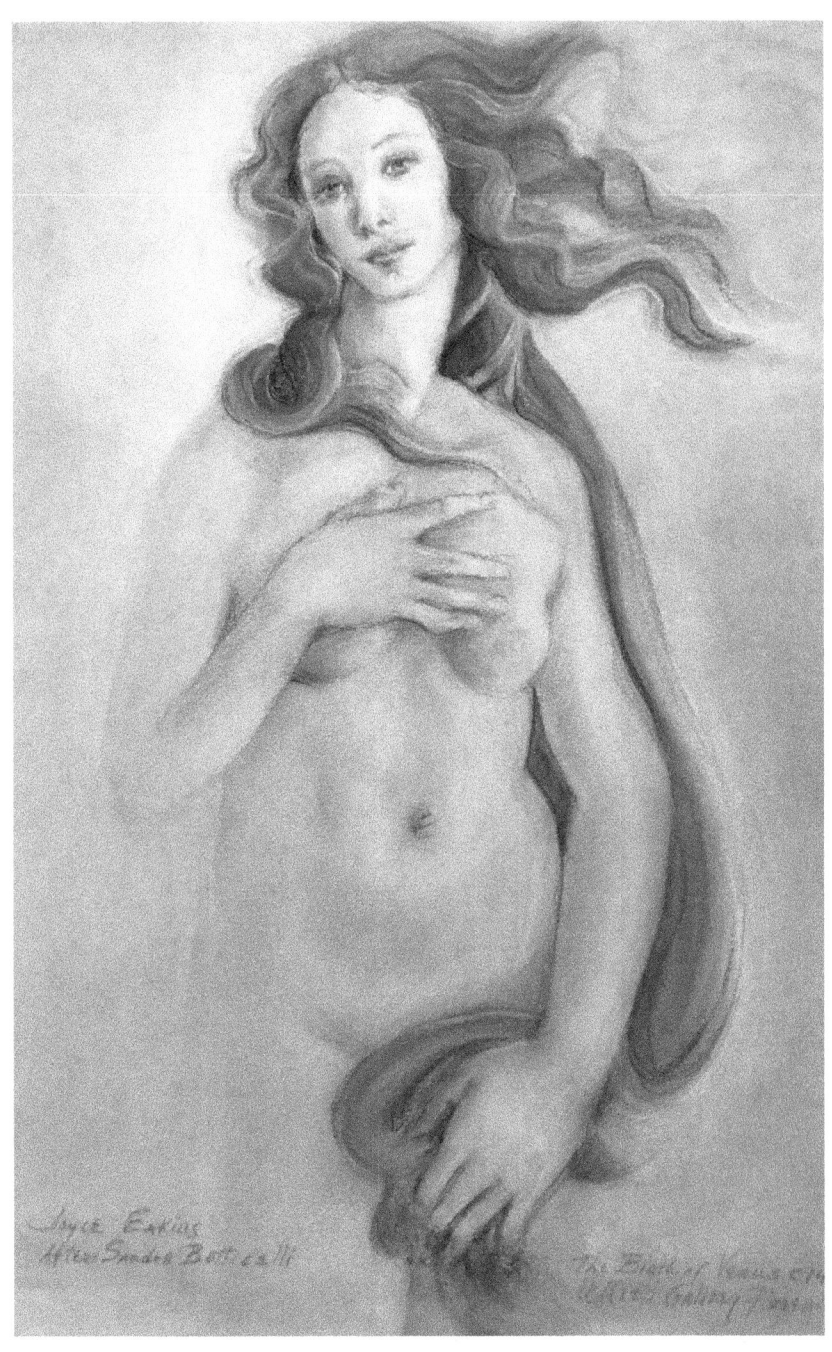

Joyce Eakins
After Sandro Botticelli

The Birth of Venus c.1486
Uffizi Gallery, Florence

Joyce Eakins
After Peter Paul Rubens (1577-1640)
Study of River God
Victoria and Albert Museum, London

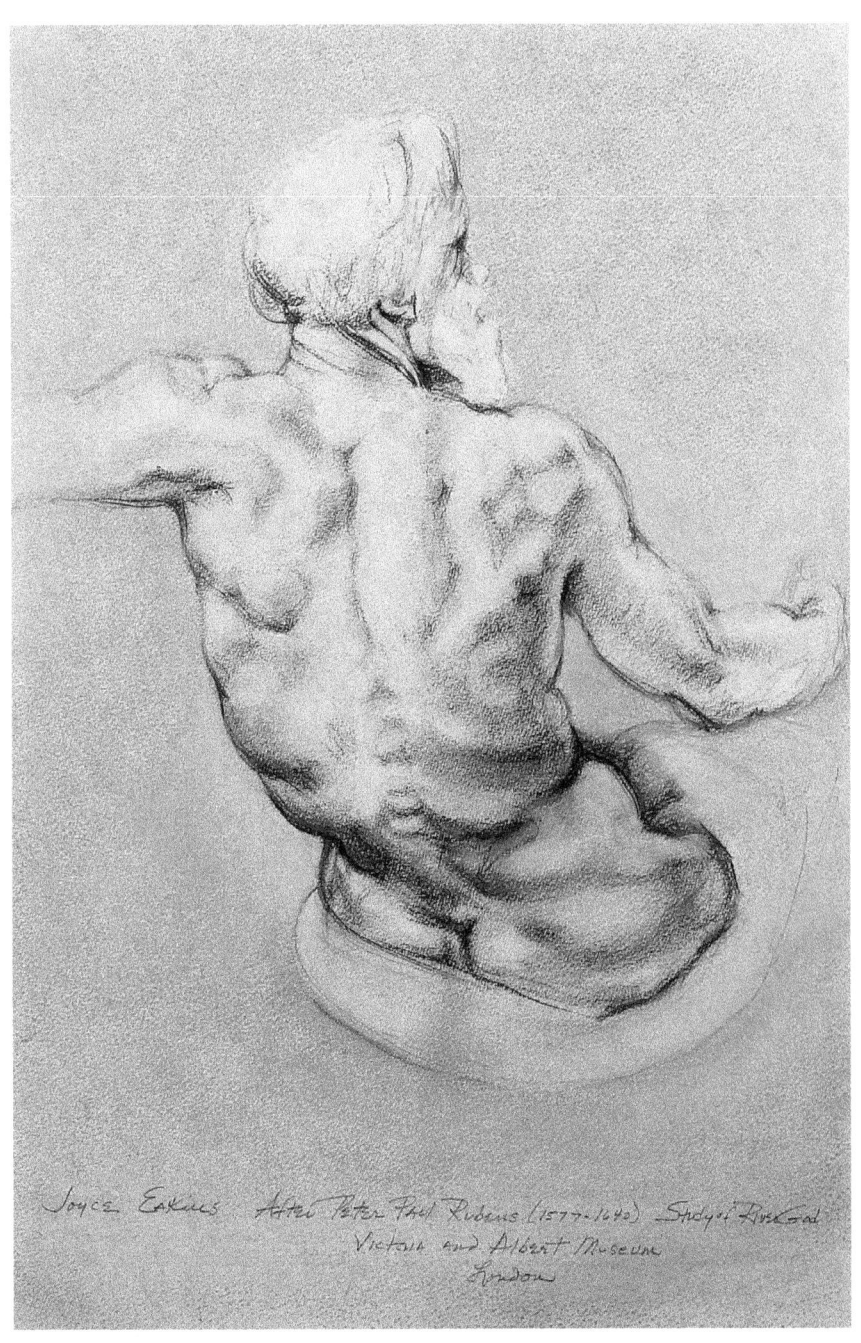

Joyce Eakins   After Peter Paul Rubens (1577-1640) Study: River God
Victoria and Albert Museum
London

Joyce Eakins
After Peter Paul Rubens (1577-1640)
Mary Magdalene
British Museum, London

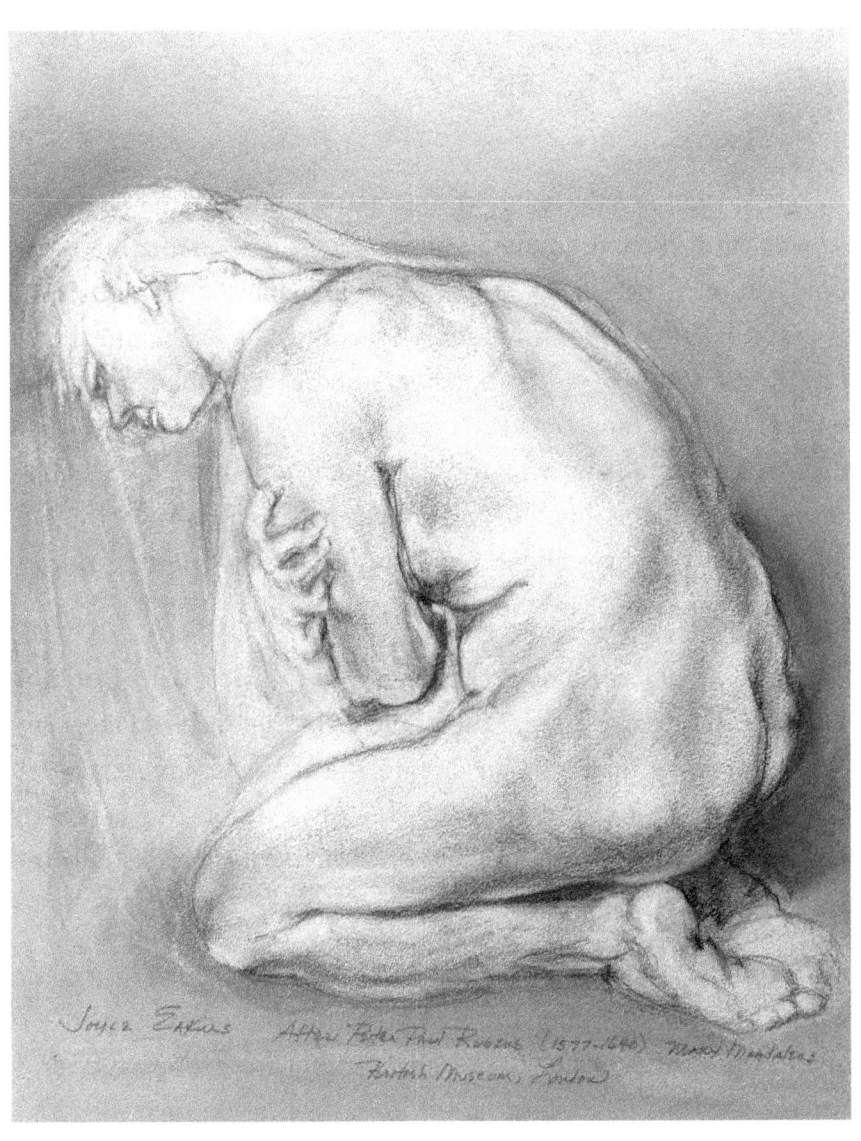

Joyce Eakins   After Peter Paul Rubens (1577-1640) Mary Magdalene
British Museum, London

The Power of Music

At the Museum of Cycladic Art in Athens, a sculpture, shaped like a viola and likened to the human body, jumped out at me. I bought the replica I look at now. The original was created 5,300 years ago. In 1914 Picasso made a breakthrough in sculpture with his "La Guitare," a piece that bears some resemblance to that ancient one. At museums in Turkey and Greece, I saw flutes and drums that dated back to the Stone Age. In the womb babies resonate with the beat of their mother's heart. At birth they inhale their first breath and exhale their first cry, music to every mother's ears. Music is inherent in our nature.

I believe the physical body resonates with the vibrations from the Big Bang, the primal sound, the original cry that inspired creation. The resounding quality is an infinite re-call, a reminder to wake up, to reconnect. Intuitively, I feel the lure, the haunting enticement to return to the point of origin—where exists only the sound of universal harmony.

I feel the persistent striving to understand when I tune into some of the jazz improvisations of Keith Jarrett. He wrestles with the angels again and again. Each repeated phrase probes the edge with ever more passionate intensity until the journey ends in a victorious break through. Spiraling full circle, he finds a place of harmony an octave higher. Home at last, we're free to fall in love all over again.

Years ago, accompanied by a Beethoven symphony, I created a painting I called "Come Ride with Me." The power of Beethoven's music was the dominant force—the magnet that attracted me. My soul rode heaving waves before being swallowed in the turbulent sea. Murky skies exploded with unpredictable streaks of lights and darks. The anguish ended in euphoric applause—the universal struggle conquered—the painting finished.

That painting became one of 75 paintings exhibited at the Taipei Fine Arts Museum, Taiwan Republic of China. The paintings were chosen to express the recent art trends in American Art in 1970. After closure, the exhibition traveled to France and was shown at Chateau de Tours, Tours, France.

Leo Tolstoy, the Russian writer, referred to music as the universal language of the emotions. My body, soul, and spirit never fail to stop and listen as Bach's "Air on a G String" wafts through the air. The sound resonates in my soul—instantly transforming my mood. When I watch my favorite movie, Casa Blanca, tears of pride and patriotism well up every time I hear the French National Anthem. Emotions are universal. I feel them in my body. I understand them in my soul.

When I was twelve years old, I went to Guiseppi Verdi's opera "Rigoletto." I felt like I had been struck by lightning when the soprano sang a high note. What I had been struck by was the power of music. The sound penetrated my heart—instantly flooding my whole being with love. Many years later I learned that sound was C# over high C.

During a visit with my mother at an assisted living center I observed an elderly gentleman seated in a tall backed wing-chair. His head rested against one of the wings. His arms hung limply over the sides his fingers nearly touching the floor. His skin was transparent. His eyes were closed. His breath was indiscernible.

Hunched in a chair across the room, a tiny lady—I guessed to be in her nineties—slowly stood up and walked unsteadily toward a piano. Sitting down she placed her quivering hands on the keys. Out of those arthritic fingers drifted old familiar tunes. The man in the chair never moved his head, nor did he open his eyes. He had the demeanor of death. Then almost imperceptibly the fingers of one hand began to move in time with the music. The sound had touched his heart and awakened his soul. I saw the power of music.

Like a radio wave—with my dial tuned to a specific frequency—I resonate with whatever I'm in accord with. The vibratory level is the magnet that either draws me in or attracts something to me. I take the "A" train with Duke Ellington, or travel the high road with Bach. I might be enticed by a Michelangelo drawing, or a Rothko painting. At the core of the attraction is a shared commonality, a binding force, the medium of connection. Whether it be art, music, or family, my life is formed by these connections.

After Thoughts

Drawing opens the door. A sudden leap—I'm absorbed in experience. I'm here, I'm now, I'm one. With no division—I'm outside of time—inside of love. When I'm there I never want to be any other place.

Love is the urgency, the attraction, the allurement, the invisible bridge, the connecting force that integrates opposites. Love is the universal drive, the compelling power that prods and persuades me. It *wakes me up* more and more to the unrealized— unimaginable—never to be fully understood potential of the human body, mind, and spirit, and to all life as well.

The relentless insistence to *wake up*—to understand my own nature—is a gift and a goad that will never be satisfied. I'm forever grateful for this tenacious benevolence, that never wearies of attempting to shake me awake. Little by little, as I *wake up* to Mother Nature's original intention, something more of true nature will show itself: *The invisible will become a little more felt.*

The answer to those age-old questions: "Who am I? Why am I? Where am I going?" could be— *I'm there. I just have to WAKE UP AND LOVE! That is the essence, that is the invisible reality—if I see rightly.*

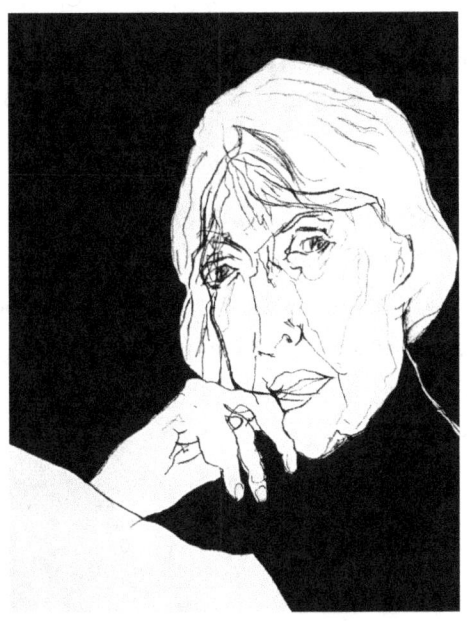

Joyce Eakins, M.F.A.

"Do what you love and love what you do." That's what I tell myself and that's what I told every student I taught. I started teaching when I was in graduate school and continued for over thirty years. During that time I served as Chairperson of the Fine Arts Department at Colorado Women's College. Subsequently, I taught at the Women's College of the University of Denver.

My work has been exhibited in traveling exhibits in the U.S.A. and internationally and has shown in the Watercolor U.S.A. National Invitational Exhibit, the National Art Club of New York, the Butler Institute of American Art, the Palm Springs Desert Museum, the Laguna Beach Art Gallery in addition to other galleries and museums.

My paintings appear in *Watercolor Bold and Free* by Lawrence Goldsmith, *Watercolor: See for Yourself* by Mary Carhartt, and *Tarot of the Spirit* created by my daughter, Pamela Eakins, and me, published by U. S. Games, Inc. and Samuel Weiser/Red Wheel Press, Inc.

For the past five years, my fascination with the human body has taken form in drawing from life, as well as writing about the experience. Each of us lives inside our own skin—our home inside our home. It's curiosity that draws me into the invisible world—the world within. Life is a curious thing. What could be a more relevant subject.

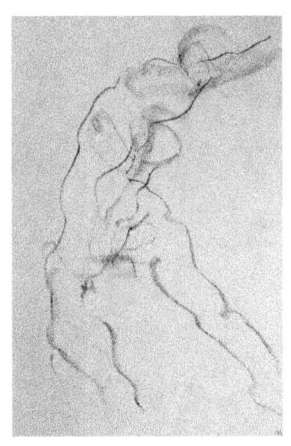

A Search for the Invisible

www.ingramcontent.com/pod-product-compliance
Lightning Source LLC
Chambersburg PA
CBHW071303220526
45468CB00001B/249